teacher's friend
publications

NOVEMBER

a creative idea book
for the
elementary teacher

written and illustrated

by

Karen Sevaly

Edited by Shelley Price

Copyright © 1986, 1997
Teacher's Friend Publications, Inc.
All rights reserved.
Printed in the United States of America
Published by Teacher's Friend Publications, Inc.
3240 Trade Center Dr., Riverside, CA 92507

ISBN 0-439-50379-5

This book is dedicated
to teachers and children
everywhere.

Table of Contents

Making the most of it!

WHAT IS IN THIS BOOK:

You will find the following in each monthly idea book from Teacher's Friend Publications:

1. A calendar listing every day of the month with a classroom idea and mention of special holidays and events.

2. At least four student awards to be sent home to parents.

3. Three or more bookmarks that can be used in your school library or given to students by you as "Super Student Awards.

4. Numerous bulletin board ideas and patterns pertaining to the particular month and seasonal activity.

5. Easy-to-make craft ideas related to the monthly holidays and special days.

6. Dozens of activities emphasizing not only the obvious holidays but also the often forgotten celebrations such as Children's Book Week and Election Day.

7. Creative writing pages, crossword puzzles, word finds, bookle covers, games, paper bag puppets, literature lists and much more!

8. Scores of classroom management techniques and methods proven to motivate your students to improve behavior and classroom work.

HOW TO USE THIS BOOK:

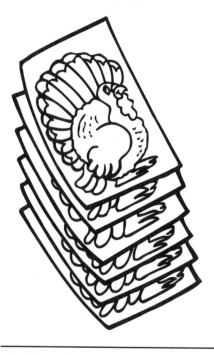

Every page of this book may be duplicated for individual class-room use.

Some pages are meant to be copied or used as duplicating masters. Other pages may be transferred onto construction paper or used as they are.

If you have access to a print shop, you will find that many pages work well when printed on index paper. This type of paper takes crayons and felt markers well and is sturdy enough to last. (Bookmarks work particularly well on index paper.)

Lastly, some pages are meant to be enlarged with an overhead or opaque projector. When we say enlarge, we mean it! Think BIG! Three, four or even five feet is great! Try using colored butcher paper or poster board so you don't spend all your time coloring.

MONTHLY ORGANIZERS:

Staying organized month after month, year after year can be a real challenge. Try this simple idea:

After using the loose pages from this book, file them in their own file folder labeled with the month's name. This will also provide a place to save pages from other reproducible books along with craft ideas, recipes and articles you find in magazines and periodicals. (*Essential Pocket Folders* by Teacher's Friend provide a perfect way to store your monthly ideas and reproducibles. Each *Monthly Essential Pocket Folder* comes with a sixteen-page booklet of essential patterns and organizational ideas. There are even special folders for *Back to School, The Substitute Teacher* and *Parent-Teacher Conferences.*)

You might also like to dedicate a file box for every month of the school year. A covered box will provide room to store large patterns, sample art projects, certificates and awards, monthly stickers, monthly idea books and much more.

BULLETIN BOARDS IDEAS:

Creating clever bulletin boards for your classroom need not take fantastic amounts of time and money. With a little preparation and know-how, you can have different boards each month with very little effort. Try some of these ideas:

1. Background paper should be put up only once a year. Choose colors that can go with many themes and holidays. The black butcher paper background you used as a spooky display in October will have a special dramatic effect in April with student-made, paper-cut butterflies.

2. Butcher paper is not the only thing that can be used to cover the back of your board. You might also try fabric from a colorful bed sheet or gingham material. Just fold it up at the end of the year to reuse again. Wallpaper is another great background cover. Discontinued rolls can be purchased for a small amount at discount hardware stores. Most can be wiped clean and will not fade like construction paper. (Do not glue wallpaper directly to the board; just staple or pin in place.)

3. Store your bulletin board pieces in large, flat envelopes made from two large sheets of tagboard or cardboard. Simply staple three sides together and slip the pieces inside. (Small pieces can be stored in zip-lock, plastic bags.) Label your large envelopes with the name of the bulletin board and the month and year you displayed it. Take a picture of each bulletin board display. Staple the picture to your storage envelope. Next year when you want to create the same display, you will know right where everything goes. Kids can even follow your directions when you give them a picture to look at.

ADDING THE COLOR:

Putting the color to finished items can be a real bother to teacher in a rush. Try these ideas:

1. On small areas, watercolor markers work great. If your area is rather large, switch to crayons or even colored chalk or pastels.

   (Don't worry, lamination or a spray fixative will keep color on the work and off of you. No laminator or fixative? That's okay, a little hair spray will do the trick.)

2. The quickest method of coloring large items is to start with colored paper. (Poster board, butcher paper or large construction paper work well.) Add a few dashes of a contrasting colored marker or crayon and you will have it made.

3. Try cutting character eyes, teeth, etc. from white typing paper and gluing them in place. These features will really stand out and make your bulletin boards come alive.

   For special effects, add real buttons or lace. Metallic paper looks great on stars and belt buckles, too.

LAMINATION:

If you have access to a roll laminator, then you already know how fortunate you are. They are priceless when it comes to saving time and money. Try these ideas:

1. You can laminate more than just classroom posters and construction paper. Try various kinds of fabric, wallpaper and gift wrapping. You'll be surprised at the great combinations you come up with.

   Laminated classified ads can be used to cut headings for current events bulletin boards. Colorful gingham fabric makes terrific cut letters or bulletin board trim. You might even try burlap! Bright foil gift wrapping paper will add a festive feeling to any bulletin board.

   (You can even make professional looking bookmarks with laminated fabric or burlap. They are great holiday gift ideas for Mom or Dad!)

2. Felt markers and laminated paper or fabric can work as a team. Just make sure the markers you use are permanent and not water-based. Oops, make a mistake! That's okay. Put a little ditto fluid on a tissue, rub across the mark and presto, it's gone! Also, dry transfer markers work great on lamination and can easily be wiped off.

LAMINATION:
(continued)

3. Laminating cut-out characters can be tricky. If you have enlarged an illustration onto poster board, simply laminate first and then cut it out with scissors or an art knife. (Just make sure the laminator is hot enough to create a good seal.)

One problem may arise when you paste an illustration onto poster board and laminate the finished product. If your paste-up is not 100% complete, your illustration and posterboard may separate after laminating. To avoid this problem, paste your illustration onto poster board that measures slightly larger than the illustration. This way, the lamination will help hold down your paste-up.

4. When pasting up your illustration, always try to use either rubber cement, artist's spray adhesive or a glue stick. White glue, tape or paste does not laminate well because it can often be seen under your artwork.

5. Have you ever laminated student-made place mats, crayon shavings, tissue paper collages, or dried flowers? You'll be amazed at the variety of creative things that can be laminated and used in the classroom or as take-home gifts.

PHOTOCOPIES AND DITTO MASTERS:

Many of the pages in this book can be copied for use in the classroom. Try some of these ideas for best results:

1. If the print from the back side of your original comes through the front when making a photocopy or ditto master, slip a sheet of black construction paper behind the sheet. This will mask the unwanted shadows and create a much better copy.

2. Several potential masters in this book contain instructions for the teacher. Simply cover the type with correction fluid or a small slip of paper before duplicating.

3. When using a new ditto master, turn down the pressure on the duplicating machine. As the copies become light, increase the pressure. This will get longer wear out of both the master and the machine.

4. Trying to squeeze one more run out of that worn ditto master can be frustrating. Try lightly spraying the inked side of the master with hair spray. For some reason, this helps the master put out those few extra copies.

LETTERING AND HEADINGS:

Not every school has a letter machine that produces perfect 4" letters. The rest of us will just have to use the old stencil-and-scissor method. But wait, there is an easier way!

1. Don't cut individual letters as they are difficult to pin up straight, anyway. Instead, hand print bulletin board titles and headings onto strips of colored paper. When it is time for the board to come down, simply roll it up to use again next year. If you buy your own pre-cut lettering, save yourself some time and hassle by pasting the desired statements onto long strips of colored paper. Laminate if possible. These can be rolled up and stored the same way!

   Use your imagination! Try cloud shapes and cartoon bubbles. They will all look great.

2. Hand lettering is not that difficult, even if your printing is not up to penmanship standards. Print block letters with a felt marker. Draw big dots at the end of each letter. This will hide any mistakes and add a charming touch to the overall effect.

   If you are still afraid to freehand it, try this nifty idea: Cut a strip of poster board about 28" X 6". Down the center of the strip, cut a window with an art knife measuring 20" X 2". There you have it: a perfect stencil for any lettering job. All you need to do is write capital letters with a felt marker within the window slot. Don't worry about uniformity. Just fill up the entire window height with your letters. Move your poster-board strip along as you go. The letters will always remain straight and even because the poster board window is straight.

3. If you must cut individual letters, use construction paper squares measuring 4 1/2" X 6". (Laminate first if you can.) Cut the capital letters as shown. No need to measure; irregular letters will look creative and not messy.

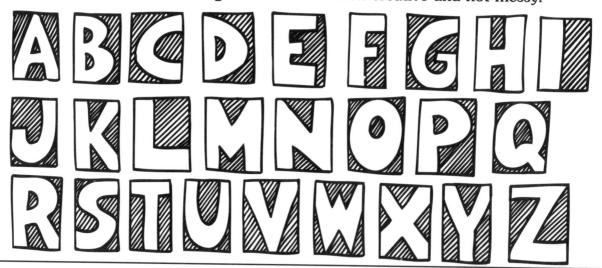

Calendar

November!

NOVEMBER

1ST   Today is AUTHOR'S DAY! (Have your students write a letter to their favorite author in honor of this day.)

2ND   DANIEL BOONE, famous American explorer and pioneer, was born on this day in 1734. (Suggest to your students that they read a book about Boone at the school library.)

3RD   Earl of Sandwich JOHN MONTAGUE, the supposed creator of the sandwich, was born on this day in 1718. (Ask your students to write a short paragraph describing in detail their favorite sandwich.)

4TH   Today marks the birthdate of American humorist WILL ROGERS, in 1879. (Read a few famous quotes by Will Roger's to your students.)

5TH   England's GUY FAWKES DAY has been celebrated on this day since 1905. (Ask students to research the reason the British celebrate this day.)

6TH   JOHN PHILIP SOUSA, America's "March King," was born on this day in 1854. (Play some of his inspirational music for your students. Primary children might like to march to the music.)

7TH   American explorers LEWIS and CLARK reached the Pacific Ocean on this day in 1805. (Ask students to find out the name of the Indian woman that guided them on their journey.)

8TH   EDMUND HALLEY, famous English astronomer and the first to predict the appearance of a comet, was born on this day in 1656. (Ask students to research comets and describe what was learned from Halley's comet in 1985.)

9TH   Nobel prize-winning physicist MARIE CURIE was born on this day in 1867. (Ask students to find out about her discovery.)

10TH   German religious reformer MARTIN LUTHER was born on this day in 1483. (Martin Luther began one of our most cherished Christmas traditions. Ask students to discover which one.)

11TH Today marks the traditional observance of VETERAN'S DAY, formally ARMISTICE DAY. (Have students observe a moment of silence in honor of America's war veterans.)

12TH Today marks the birthdate of ELIZABETH CADY STANTON, a leader of the women's suffrage movement in America in 1815. (Discuss the changes that have taken place in the women's movement in recent years.)

13TH Scottish poet and novelist ROBERT LOUIS STEVENSON was born on this day in 1850. (Read a poem or two to your students from Stevenson's <u>A Child's Garden of Verses</u>.)

14TH ROBERT FULTON, American inventor of the steamboat, was born on this day in 1765. (Ask students to find out how his invention changed American transportation and industry.)

15TH SCHICHI-GO-SAN is celebrated today in Japan. On this day, children visit shrines and offer gifts of thanksgiving. (Ask students to locate Japan on the classroommap.)

16TH Today is SADIE HAWKINS' DAY. "Women first" is the rule of the day. (Let the girls of your class be first toda:, first on the bus, first on the playground, first to go to lunch, etc.)

17TH The SUEZ CANAL in Egypt was opened on this day in 1869. (Ask students to find the Suez Canal on the classroom map and discuss the importance of this waterway in world trade.)

18TH Today marks the birthdate of MICKEY MOUSE in 1928. (Ask students to find out which cartoon was Mickey's first.)

19TH Today is DISCOVERY DAY in Puerto Rico. Christopher Columbus discovered this island in 1493. (Teach your students to say "Hello" *(Buenos Dias)*, "Goodbye" *(Adios)* and "Thank you" *(Gracias)* in Spanish.)

20TH PEREGRINE WHITE, the first child born in the colonies of English parents, was born on this day in 1620. (Discuss with your students the hardships that befell the pilgrims during that first winter.)

21ST Today is WORLD HELLO DAY! (Teach your students to say hello in three or four different languages.

22ND U.S. President JOHN F. KENNEDY was assassinated on this day in 1963. (Display books about Kennedy's life in the silent reading area of your classroom.)

23RD   FRANKLIN PIERCE the 14th President of the United States was born on this day in 1804. (Pierce never wanted to be President. Ask students to find out more about this President.)

24TH   FATHER JUNIPERO SERRA, founder of the California missions, was born on this day in 1713. (Ask students to trace his mission route and locate his missions along the California coast using the classroom map.)

25TH   American industrialist ANDREW CARNEGIE was born on this day in 1835. (Carnegie gave away most of his wealth to worthy charities and causes. Ask students to research his accomplishments.)

26TH   Today is SOJOURNER TRUTH MEMORIAL DAY. (Have students honor this early civil rights leader by finding out more about her life and accomplishments.)

27TH   American architect HENRY BACON was born on this day in 1866. (Ask students to find out which historical monuments and buildings were designed by Bacon.)

28TH   The first UNITED STATES POST OFFICE opened its doors on this day in 1783. (Ask students to learn their zip codes in commemoration.)

29TH   American novelist LOUISA MAY ALCOTT was born on this day in 1832. (Suggest her book <u>Little Women</u> for student reading during Children's Book Week.)

30TH   SAMUEL CLEMENS, American author and humorist was born on this day in 1835. (Ask students to find out the pen name that Clemens used.

DON'T FORGET THESE OTHER IMPORTANT HOLIDAYS:

ELECTION DAY   (The first Tuesday in November.)

THANKSGIVING DAY   (The fourth Thursday in November.)

CHILDREN'S BOOK WEEK   (The third week of November.)

November Calendar Symbols

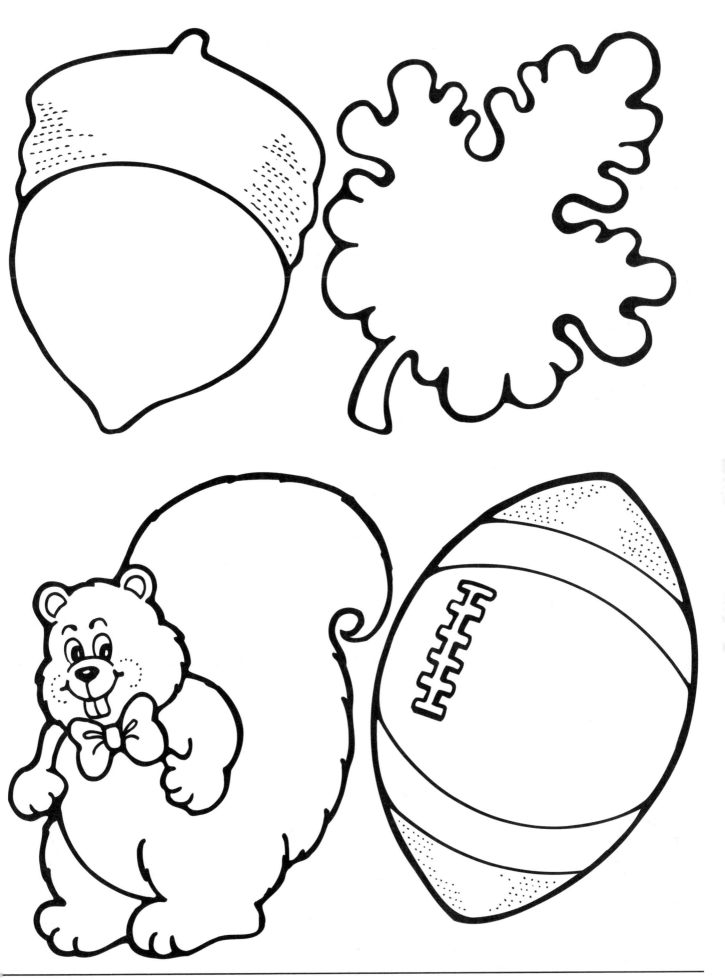

November

Sunday	Monday	Tuesday	Wednesday	Thursday	Friday	Saturday

Harvest Activities!

Harvest Festivals!

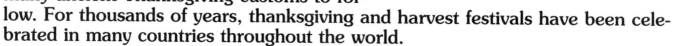

In the United States, Thanksgiving has always been viewed as a uniquely American holiday. Our first Thanksgiving was observed by the English Pilgrims in the year 1621. The Pilgrims, however, had many ancient Thanksgiving customs to follow. For thousands of years, thanksgiving and harvest festivals have been celebrated in many countries throughout the world.

The following descriptions of harvest festivals and their countries of origin can be used as a base for class discussion.

GREECE

"Harvest to the Goddess Demeter" - The ancient Greeks made yearly offerings to Demeter the goddess of the soil. This feasting time was so highly regarded that it was held even during times of war. During the celebration, soldiers would cease fighting and joyfully march through the streets carrying stalks of grain. This three-day festival was held in the month of November.

ACTIVITY - Introduce your students to many of the characters in Greek mythology and legends. Have your students locate Greece on the classroom map.

ISRAEL

"Sukkot" or "Hebrew Feast of the Tabernacles" - This Jewish harvest festival falls in the month of September or October. During Sukkot, Jewish families build small huts or tents to represent the dwellings their ancestors used while living in the wilderness. Traditionally, family members lay leafy tree branches across the open roofs and decorate the small huts with flowers and fruits. This is a great day for feasting and thanking God for the harvest.

ACTIVITY - Create your own fruit-filled centerpiece in honor of Sukkot. Let your students sample the various fruits of the season such as apples, grapes, figs, dates and even pomegranates.

FRANCE

"Wheat Harvest Festival" - During the last week of August, rural people of France celebrate their plentiful wheat harvest. Farmers decorate their tractors and parade them down the village streets for all to enjoy. Visitors can see demonstrations of the separation of the wheat and chaff and observe the process by which grain is ground into flour. The aroma of fresh baked bread fills the air as people buy loaves of bread made from the local flour.

ACTIVITY - Using a portable bread maker, let your students experience smelling and eating fresh, homemade bread in the classroom. You might even try some exotic varieties such as rye, sourdough, cinnamon-raisin, or pumpernickel.

Harvest Festivals!

CHINA

"Harvest Moon Festival" - This harvest festival is also known as the birthday of the moon. This is a special time of feasting and honoring the moon goddess. Legend states that the moon goddess grants wishes during the moon festival. In celebration, Chinese women bake traditional "moon cakes." One year during a war, village women baked messages into the "moon cakes" that were then delivered to the soldiers. These "moon cake" messages helped them defeat their enemy.

ACTIVITY - Ask students to each write a special wish on a small slip of paper using permanent ink. Tell them to fold the paper very small. Make muffins in the classroom by following the directions on a package muffin mix. Fill the muffin cups about one-third with batter, place a folded wish paper in each cup and fill it with the remaining batter. Bake as directed. Give each student a muffin to eat and ask them to read the wish inside.

ENGLAND

"Harvest Home" - Worshippers throughout England observe this lovely festival by decorating their churches with flowers, fruits, grains and vegetables. The food is later donated to the poor. Often, people from entire villages follow the last harvest wagon in from the fields. They walk behind the wagon throughout the town singing songs and hymns.

ACTIVITY - Encourage children to bring from home non-perishable foods that can be donated to a worthy charity or needy family. Collect the canned foods in a large basket or student-decorated box. Children can also write notes to the recipients wishing them well.

IROQUOIS NATION

"Harvest Ceremony" - The Iroquois tribes celebrated the spirits of many fruits and various crops. They particularly observed and gave thanks for strawberries, raspberries and corn. They observed their thanksgiving with prayers for future great harvests.

ACTIVITY - Have students collect a variety of food labels, noting products whose ingredients contain corn. Students will be surprised to see how many of their favorite foods contain corn syrup, corn meal and corn starch.

CHEROKEE NATION

"Itse Selu" or "Harvest Festival" - During the ripening of the corn, the Cherokee people show appreciation for this most important crop by devoting four days to its celebration. At sundown, children gather to hear the elders tell Indian legends and wonderful tales.

ACTIVITY - Let students research various Indian tales in the school library and orally report about the legends in front of the class.

Corn Husk Pattern

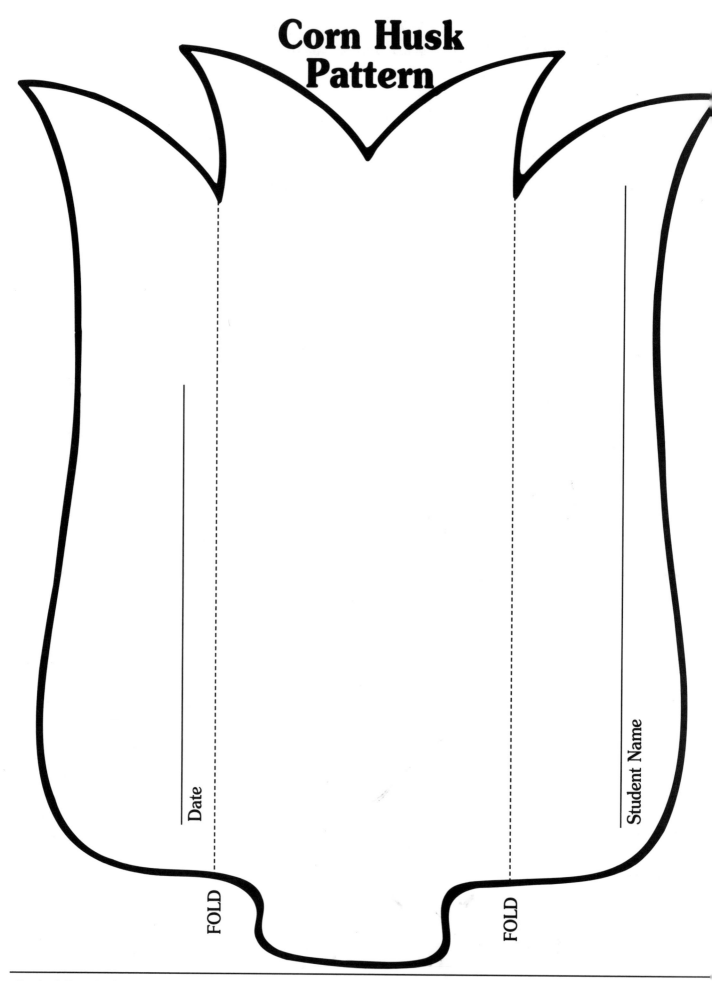

Date

FOLD

Student Name

FOLD

Reading Harvest

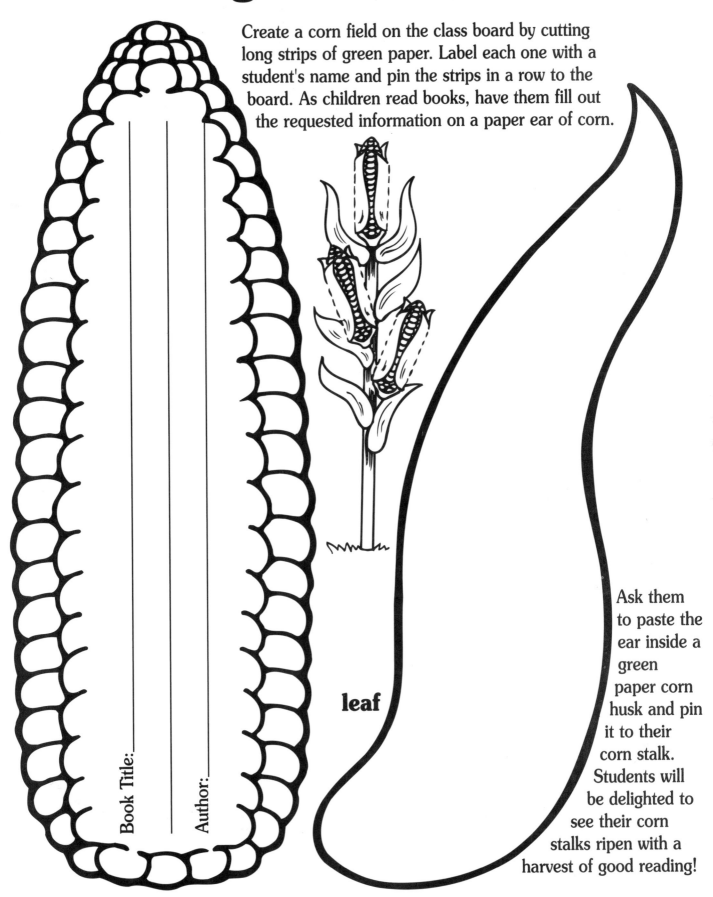

Create a corn field on the class board by cutting long strips of green paper. Label each one with a student's name and pin the strips in a row to the board. As children read books, have them fill out the requested information on a paper ear of corn.

leaf

Book Title:

Author:

Ask them to paste the ear inside a green paper corn husk and pin it to their corn stalk. Students will be delighted to see their corn stalks ripen with a harvest of good reading!

Don't be a Turkey!

READ!

Name

Don't Forget to Vote!

Name

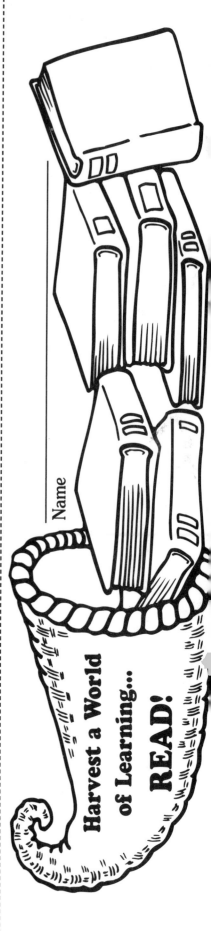

Name

Harvest a World of Learning...

READ!

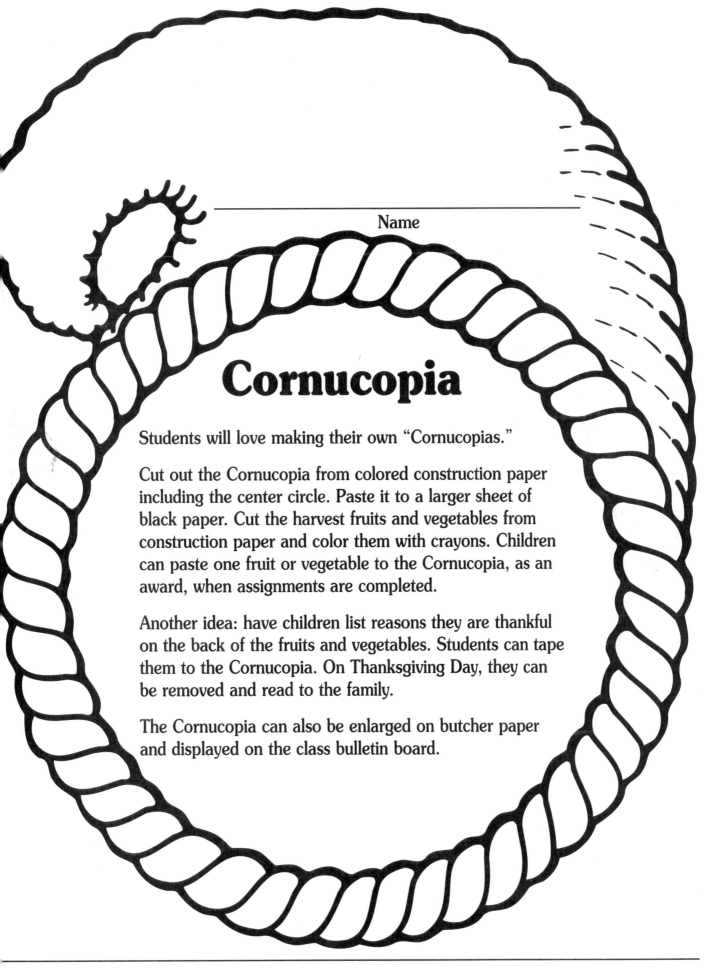

_____

Name

Cornucopia

Students will love making their own "Cornucopias."

Cut out the Cornucopia from colored construction paper including the center circle. Paste it to a larger sheet of black paper. Cut the harvest fruits and vegetables from construction paper and color them with crayons. Children can paste one fruit or vegetable to the Cornucopia, as an award, when assignments are completed.

Another idea: have children list reasons they are thankful on the back of the fruits and vegetables. Students can tape them to the Cornucopia. On Thanksgiving Day, they can be removed and read to the family.

The Cornucopia can also be enlarged on butcher paper and displayed on the class bulletin board.

Harvest Patterns

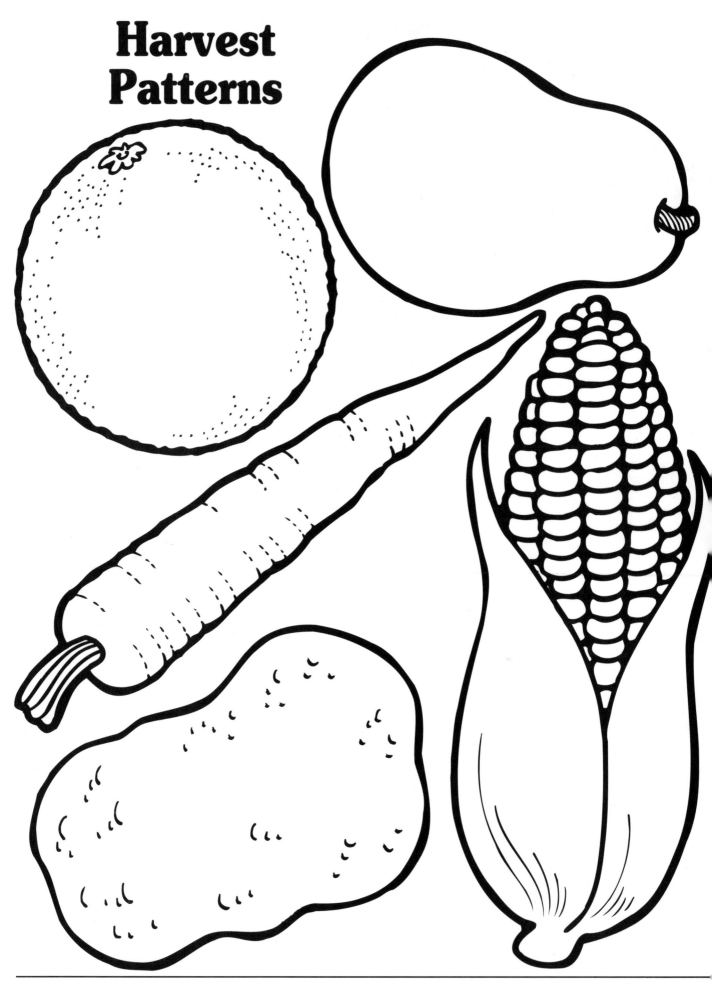

Pencil Toppers

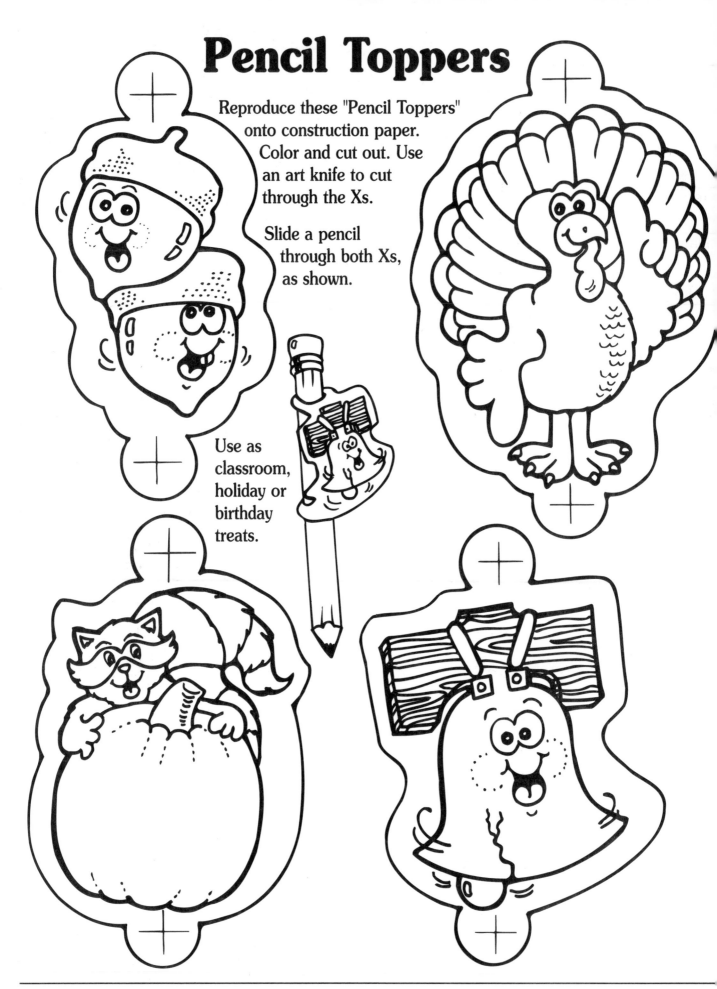

Reproduce these "Pencil Toppers" onto construction paper. Color and cut out. Use an art knife to cut through the Xs.

Slide a pencil through both Xs, as shown.

Use as classroom, holiday or birthday treats.

_____
Name

harvested a bunch of learning today!

_____
Teacher

_____
Date

Much Better!

_____
Name

_____
Teacher

_____
Date

_____
Name

Really Did a Great Job Today!

_____
Date

_____
Teacher

WOW!

Look who was a terrific student!

_____
Name

_____

_____

_____
Teacher   Date

CERTIFICATE

OF

AWARD

presented to

_____

NAME

in recognition of

_____

_____
TEACHER

_____
DATE

STUDENT OF THE MONTH

NAME

SCHOOL

DATE

TEACHER

Harvest Color Page

Woodsy Animals!

Woodsy Animal Activities!

RANGER RICK

Ranger Rick is a savvy raccoon in a ranger hat. Students may enjoy a subscription to his magazine or find out ways they can protect the local wildlife. Have them write to the following address:

Ranger Rick
Backyard Wildlife Habitat
National Wildlife Federation
1412 Sixteenth Street, N.W.
Washington, DC 20036-2266

RESEARCHING RACCOONS

Ask your students to find out about the remarkable raccoon. Here is a list of questions you might like to have them answer:

> What do they eat?
> Where do they live?
> Do they hibernate in the winter?
> How do they take care of their
>   young?
> Is there more than one type of
>   raccoon?
> Do they wash their food?
> Can they swim?
> How have humans used raccoons?
> How are raccoons harmful to
>   humans?
> Can raccoons be kept as pets?

SQUIRRELS AND CHIPMUNKS

Squirrels, chipmunks and all gnawing animals are called rodents. There are hundreds of different kinds of rodents. Other rodents include rats, mice, gophers, beavers, woodchucks and porcupines.

Rodents are mammals, meaning that they have fur, are warm-blooded and feed their babies milk from their own bodies. They are special because they are the only mammals other than man who store their food for the winter. Some rodents have pouches in their cheeks in which to stuff food so they can carry it to their hiding place.

Ask your students to find out about different rodents. Which one is the largest? Smallest? Which ones are a nuisance? Where can they be found?

THE _____ WENT OVER.....!

Teach your students the tune and words to *The Bear Went Over the Mountain*. Divide the class into several small groups and ask students to substitute different animals for the bear. The groups can perform their song in front of the class!

(Original Words)
The bear went over the mountain,
The bear went over the mountain,
The bear went over the mountain,
To see what he could see.

The other side of the mountain,
The other side of the mountain,
The other side of the mountain,
Was all that he could see.

Woodsy Animal Activities!

BACKYARD REFUGE

Students may like to provide a refuge area for local wildlife animals. You may need the help of a parent or someone that has access to the type of property that can provide the necessary habitat.

The area will need to have many plants and mature trees. Berry bushes and flowering plants will attract many birds and even bats. (You may want to add a bat house to your habitat.) Don't cut back any vegetation. Let grass grow tall and natural.

The area should have a water source such as a bird bath or small pond. The water will attract frogs, ducks and dragonflies.

A rock pile and/or a fallen tree will provide protection for lizards and chipmunks. Rabbits and raccoons need dense shrubs.

If you place bird feeders or establish other artificial ways to feed wild animals, make sure you continue throughout the cold weather months. Birds and animals become dependent upon easily acceptable food. They often starve when this food source is suddenly stopped.

REAL BEARS

Ask your students to learn a few things about real bears. You might like them to research such bears as the Grizzly Bear, Brown Bear, Black Bear and the Polar Bear. (Pandas and Koalas are marsupials, not bears.) Ask them to find out the answers to these questions:

1 How large do they grow?
2. Where do they live?
3. What do they eat?
4. What do they do in the winter?
5. How do they care for their young?
6. Are they endangered?
7. Can they be dangerous?
8. How long do they usually live?

WILDLIFE IN THE CITY

Most people think that wild animals can only be found in rural areas. However, many different animals can be found throughout and on the outskirts of most cities; you just have to look for them. Mice, rats, bats, muskrats, squirrels, raccoons, skunks, foxes and many birds and insects can all be found around cities. Here is a list of some things to look for:

Look for chewed pinecones and nuts left by squirrels and birds.

Look for tracks in muddy or sandy areas. You can identify animals by the tracks they leave. Research different animal tracks in the library.

Look for animal droppings to know if animals have been present. A pile of feathers or bones is a sure sign that some animal has had a meal.

When looking for animals, make sure you wear clothing that blends with the surroundings. Move very slowly and freeze if you think an animal is near. Make sure that you approach the area with the wind in your face so that animals won't smell you coming.

Raccoon Puppet

Cut this raccoon puppet pattern from construction paper. Glue the two pieces to a small, brown paper lunch bag.

A great way to
show off good
work papers!

Raccoon
Pattern

Display this raccoon
at the top of a sheet
of 9" x 12" construc-
tion paper. Attach the
tail to the bottom of
the sheet.

Who's Inside?

Cut open the hole in the tree and fold back. Paste the entire tree onto a sheet of construction paper. Children can draw a squirrel or chipmunk behind the opening. Or, cut a woodsy animal from the next page and glue it inside the tree opening.

Woodsy Animal Patterns

Use these cute illustrations as team mascots, clip art, student awards or as a stimulus for creative writing assignments.

Cut out

Cut out

Bear Mask

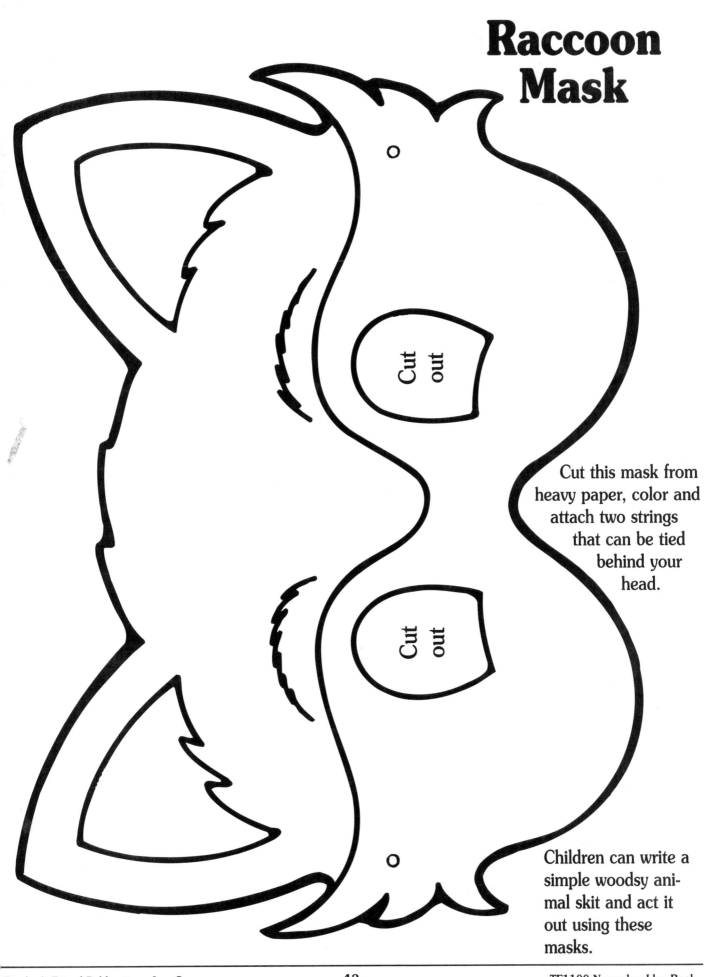

Raccoon Mask

Cut out

Cut out

Cut this mask from heavy paper, color and attach two strings that can be tied behind your head.

Children can write a simple woodsy animal skit and act it out using these masks.

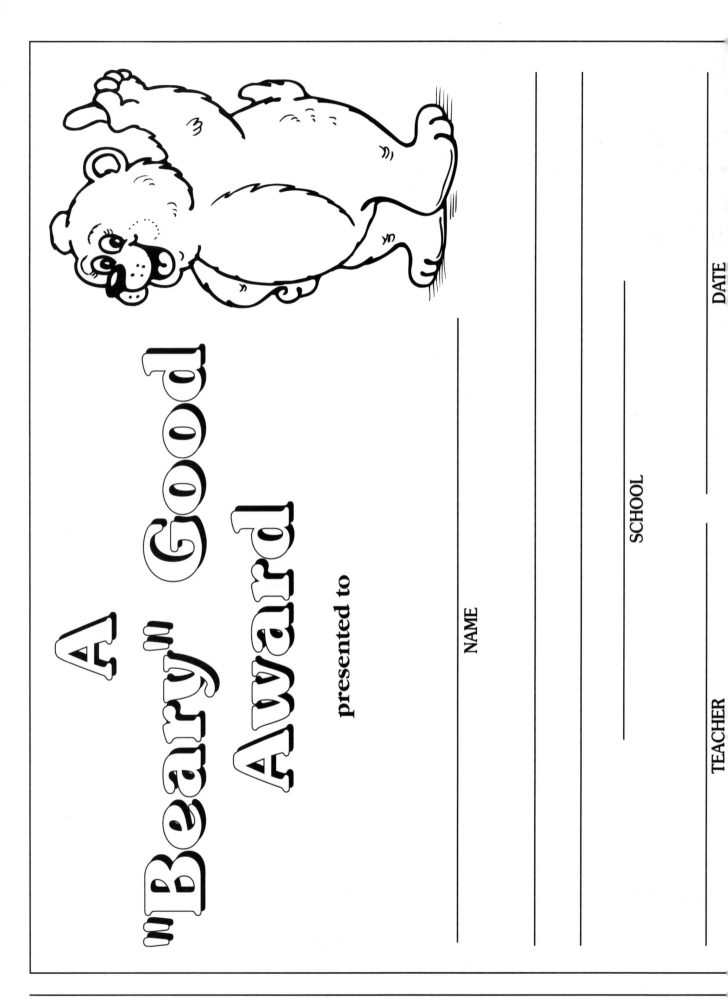

A "Beary" Good Award

presented to

NAME

SCHOOL

TEACHER

DATE

My Animal Report

Student's Name

The animal I've chosen is a ...

_____

It lives in _____

_____

_____

_____

It eats _____

_____

_____

My animal can grow to be this big:

(Draw a picture of your animal.)

List some special things about your animal.

_____

_____

_____

In the winter, my animal... _____

_____

_____

This animal is: ☐ **endangered** ☐ **not endangered**

(Write a fictional story about what would happen if you met this animal in the wild.)

FOLD

Name

Woodsy Animal Booklet

Children's Book Week!

Book Week Activities - Third Week in November

BOOKMARK CONTEST

Students will have fun designing their own bookmarks and at the same time will give the school library an abundant supply. Give each child a blank bookmark pattern. Ask students to think of a catchy jingle or saying that can be printed and then illustrated on the bookmark. Collect the bookmarks and display them in the library. A panel of teachers can judge the contest. Give prize ribbons to the top three winners. Duplicate the winning bookmarks for use by all students.

NEW BOOK JACKETS

Many books are never checked out because their jackets are worn or unattractive. Instruct students to select a book from the library that they would like to refurbish with a new book jacket. (The book must be read before jackets are made.) Jackets can be made with large sheets of construction paper. Have students draw scenes or characters from the book with crayon or colored markers. Make sure that the title and author's name are clearly labeled on both the front and spine. Laminate the book jackets, if possible. The children will love seeing their book jackets displayed along with other books in the library.

BOOK SALE

After each student has read a chosen library book instruct them to "sell" the book to the rest of the class. Students may choose to do this in a number of clever ways. Here are a few ideas:

1. Make a poster depicting a scene from the book.
2. Select another student and act out a scene from the book.
3. Write a commercial using the book's important points and present it to the class.
4. Write a song about the book and sing it to your classmates.

Encourage students to include the title of the book, author's and illustrator's names, where the book can be found and why the other classmates should "buy" this book!

BOOK EXCHANGE

Send a note home to parents and ask them to send to school two old books that can be exchanged by their child for two other books. Place all of the books you collect in a large basket. As each student accomplishes a set goal, permit him or her to choose a book from the basket to read, take home and keep. (Make sure no child receives more than two, unless you have acquired several more than you need.)

READ-A-THON!

While keeping your students' abilities and grade level in mind, determine a goal of a set number of books to be read during the school year. Prominently display an incentive chart on the class board and keep track of books read by individual students. As the class approaches the goal, plan a class party. Serve refreshments and have the children come dressed as their favorite characters. You might even like to call the local newspaper or invite a local author to visit the class on this special day!

Book Report Alternatives!

1. Choose two characters from the story and write about a conversation they might have.

2. Write a letter to a close friend recommending the book you have just read.

3. Make a list of new, unusual or interesting words or phrases found in your book.

4. Prepare a television commercial about your book. Act out the commercial for your classmates.

5. Draw a cartoon strip using characters from the book.

6. Write a different ending to the story in your book. Do you like your ending better than the author's?

7. Write ten questions which could be used to test other students' understanding of the story. Make sure you include a list of the answers.

8. Explain why you think this book will or will not be read one hundred years from now. Support your opinion by stating specific events in the story.

9. Discuss one particular episode in the story that you remember most. Describe why you think it remains so clear to you.

10. Write a letter to the author of your book. Address it to the publisher and mail it.

11. Write a ballad or song about the characters and events in your story. Set the words to the music of a popular song and sing it to the class.

12. Give a dramatic reading of a scene in the book to your classmates.

13. Describe in detail three characters from the story. List reasons why these characters would be nice to know or have as a best friend.

14. Design a poster or book jacket of your book and ask to display it in the school library.

15. Using the title of your book, write a phrase about the book for each letter in the title.

16. Draw a mural depicting the major scenes from the book.

17. After reading an informational book, make a scrapbook about the subject.

18. Write a movie script for one of the scenes in your book. You might like to act it out in front of the class with the help of other students.

Reading Keys

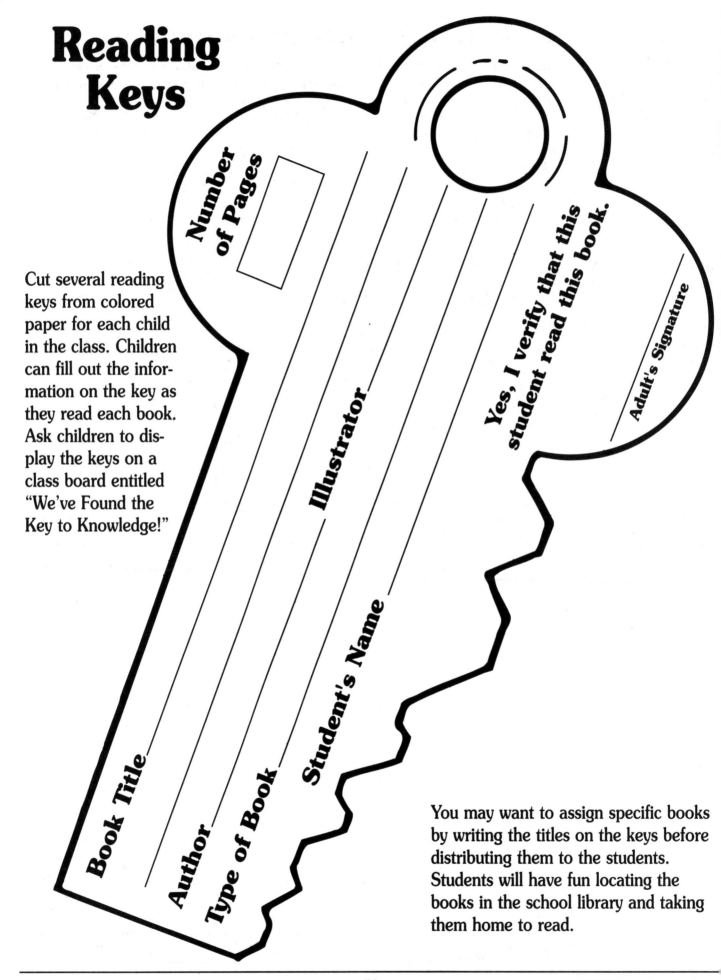

Cut several reading keys from colored paper for each child in the class. Children can fill out the information on the key as they read each book. Ask children to display the keys on a class board entitled "We've Found the Key to Knowledge!"

Number of Pages

Illustrator

Book Title

Author

Type of Book

Student's Name

Yes, I verify that this student read this book.

Adult's Signature

You may want to assign specific books by writing the titles on the keys before distributing them to the students. Students will have fun locating the books in the school library and taking them home to read.

Mr. Book Worm

Help your students learn the Dewey Decimal System with this fun activity.

Arrange with your school's librarian to conduct a library search with your students. Make several copies of this cute book worm and hide them in various books in the library. Give your students a list of clues for finding each worm's location.

An example might be:

"Mr. Book Worm has found a giant home in a peachy-keen place. The author is a real Dahl" Can you find me?"

Your students will be excited to find Roald Dahl's <u>James and the Giant Peach</u> just where it belongs in the library!

Mr. Book Worm illustration can also be used as a booklet cover or as a reading award!

Reading Connection

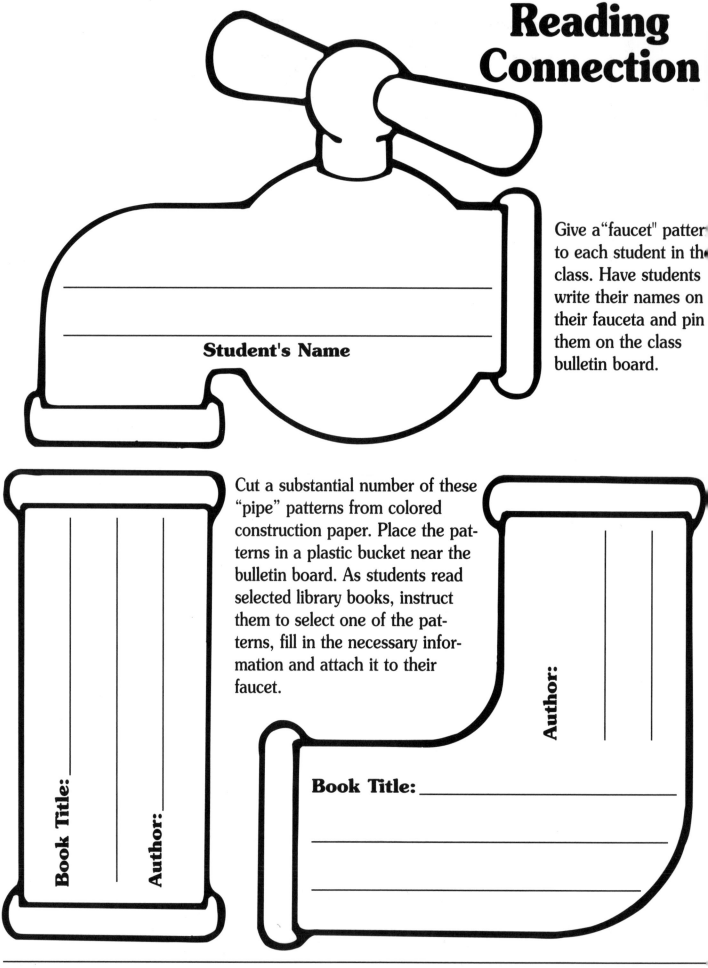

_____
Student's Name

Give a "faucet" pattern to each student in the class. Have students write their names on their fauceta and pin them on the class bulletin board.

Cut a substantial number of these "pipe" patterns from colored construction paper. Place the patterns in a plastic bucket near the bulletin board. As students read selected library books, instruct them to select one of the patterns, fill in the necessary information and attach it to their faucet.

Book Title: _____

Author: _____

Author: _____

Book Title: _____
_____
_____

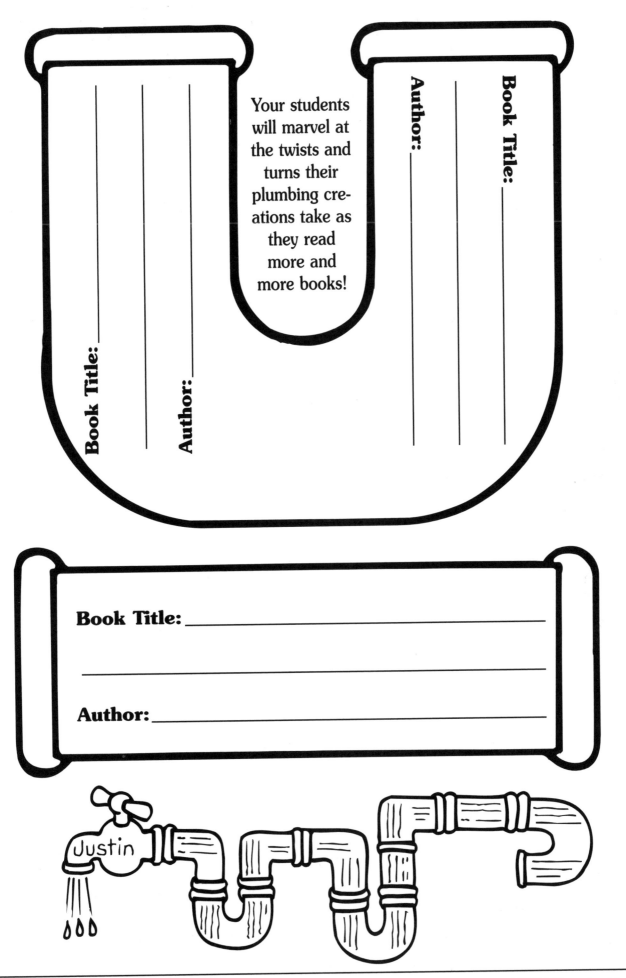

Your students will marvel at the twists and turns their plumbing creations take as they read more and more books!

Book Title: _____

Author: _____

Book Title: _____

Author: _____

Book Title: _____

Author: _____

My Book Report _____

Name

Book Title _____

Author _____

_____

_____

_____

_____

_____

_____

_____

_____

_____

_____

☐ **I liked this book.**

☐ **I didn't like this book.**

Why? _____

_____

_____

_____

READING CERTIFICATE

This award is presented to

NAME

for

DATE

TEACHER

My Reading Record _____

Name _____

Date	Book Title	Author	# of Pages Read	Parent's Initials

I've read this many pages:

A Letter Home to Parents

Dear Parents,

The reading patterns you establish at home directly influence your child's ability to do well in school. Here are a few suggestions:

LISTEN, TALK AND READ WITH YOUR CHILD

Studies show that most parents spend as little as fifteen minutes a day talking, listening and reading to their children. Yet, it is exactly these activities that encourage a child to read. The very best way to help your child become a good reader is to read to and with them at home. The more children read, or are read to, the better. Books are not the only materials they can read. Encourage your child to read cereal boxes, street signs, catalogs and magazines. Make sure that you take time out each day to read and communicate with your child.

READING AND WRITING

Teaching a child to write helps them to read. Keep pencils, paper, chalk and crayons on hand. Young children can learn to form letters and then words. This gives them the opportunity to recognize the relationship between letters and sounds. Very young children can dictate to you or to an older child. It's also fun to have children write letters to friends and family.

QUIET TIME

The work done in school is typically reinforced with homework. This gives children time to study and practice what they have learned in the classroom. It is very important to set a time for homework and to provide a quiet place where they can do their work. Remember to keep on top of your child's work and stay in touch with your child's teacher.

LIMIT TELEVISION

Most children spend hours in front of the television and only minutes a day reading. Set a limit on television watching and replace it with quality reading time. When television is permitted, follow it with family discussions.

Learning doesn't start or end at school. The more we can work together to develop good reading habits, the more successful your child will be.

(Please sign the following reading contract and have your child return it to me on the next school day.)

Sincerely,

_____

_____

Date

I promise to read _____ pages each day.
I will record my progress on my reading record.

_____

Student's Signature

_____

Parent's Signature

_____

Teacher's Signature

Step Up to Reading

Motivate your students to read by posting a "Step Up to Reading" on the class bulletin board.

Make copies of this footprint on colored paper. As a child completes a book either at home or at school, he or she receives a footprint to fill out. Students write in the information required and pin their footprints to the class board .

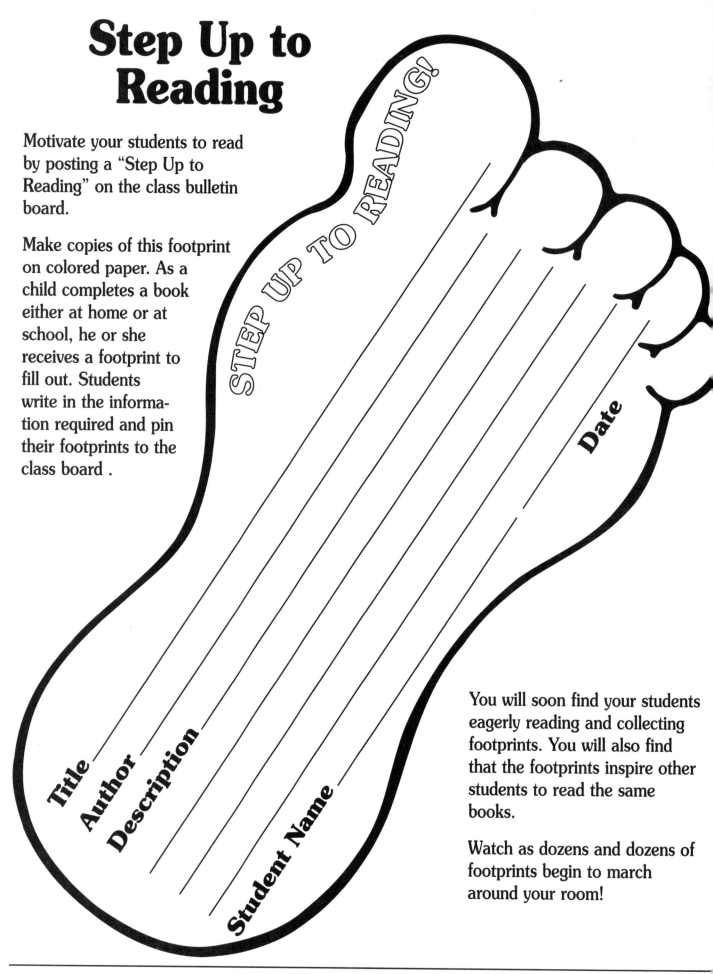

STEP UP TO READING!

Date

Title

Author

Description

Student Name

You will soon find your students eagerly reading and collecting footprints. You will also find that the footprints inspire other students to read the same books.

Watch as dozens and dozens of footprints begin to march around your room!

Election Day Activities!

Every four years, the American people vote for their choice of President of the United States. Children will be fascinated with the entire election process and eager to learn more about our presidents. Try some of these activities with your students:

CLASS DISCUSSIONS - Ask students to list various national and international issues that they think are most important. Ask them what they know of the candidate's views on these issues. Ask for students' opinions on campaign advertisements and how the methods by which money is raised to pay for them. Have students collect campaign literature that their parents receive in the mail. Display the brochures and flyers along with a sample ballot on the class bulletin board.

POLITICAL CARTOONS - Ask students to collect cartoons from local newspapers and analyze their implied messages about the election and current issues. Students might also like to research political cartoons from the past.

POLLING PLACES - Ask students to find out the location of the closest polling place closest to their homes. Polls are often located at schools. If your school contains a polling place, arrange for a visit. A poll worker may like to explain the voting process to your students. Ask students to remind their parents to vote. And don't forget to conduct a secret ballot election in your classroom.

ELECTION NIGHT - Instruct students to watch television coverage of the election results. As students watch the returns with their families, have them write the total votes from each state as they are reported. Students might like to record their findings on a U.S. map.

ELECTORAL COLLEGE - Help students understand that the president is really elected by the electoral college. In the democratic process, registered voters actually vote for electors who then vote for the president. The new president needs 270 electoral votes to win. Ask the students about the number of votes the winning candidate received in this election. Tell the students that the electorial college will meet in mid-December to finalize their vote.

ELECTION ANALYSIS - Reveal the outcome of the classroom election and discuss how it agreed with or differed from the national election. Ask students to discuss their feelings about the election. What will they most remember?
Be sure to continue with current events and discussions about the new president until Inauguration Day in January.

Election Word Find

```
S V R T G H Y K L H N S P E E C H F B N K L Y
X Z A S W Q R T H Y B H R D C V T Y H U J M H
D C X V C A N D I D A T E F H J I I L K M N G
V F G H O S X V B H L J S F T Y N A T I O N P
W R T Y N C H Y U I L N I B G H A R Y U I O P
C V G Y V H U I K J O R D S W E U C V C W Q E
Q S X D E G B F D R T U E D S W G F R A F V B
M L K O N O V E M B E R N O K J U J K M F G T
E L E C T I O N D R T Y T H N J R H G P C V B
R T Y U I S R T G H U J K I O L A G H A C X Z
L P O I O G F D E M O C R A T F T A W I D R T
S G H U N G H Y U I K M N H U Y I F T G E W Y
V I C E P R E S I D E N T F G T O F N N C E T
O F R H G B N M K I L O H B G Y N R F D E W S
T E R M C D F R E P U B L I C A N F R H Y U K
E S C V T G B N J U I K M K L O P M N J H Y T
X D R T G V B H U J M N H Y T R E W Q A S D E
F R G B N J I U H J K L O P M N B V G F R Q W
```

ACTIVITY 1

[FI]ND THESE ELECTION WORDS: NOVEMBER, PRESIDENT, VICE-PRESIDENT, VOTE, BALLOT, [D]EMOCRAT, REPUBLICAN, CANDIDATE, SPEECH, CAMPAIGN, CONVENTION, [IN]AUGURATION, ELECTION, TERM, NATION.

[U]SE THESE ELECTION WORDS IN A PARAGRAPH TO TELL WHY IT'S IMPORTANT TO VOTE!

Use these characters as election bulletin board characters or booklet covers.

Election Party Characters

DEMOCRAT

REPUBLICAN

Uncle Sam Hat

Cut this "Uncle Sam" hat from white construction paper. Have children color with crayons. Staple the hat to a strip of paper measuring the correct size to fit a child's head.

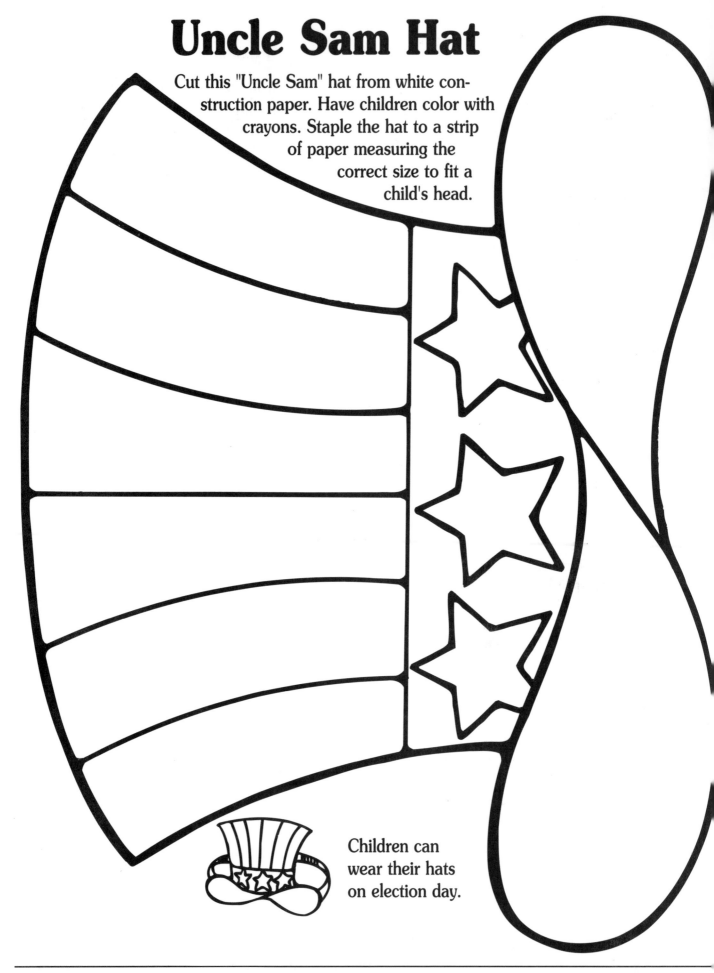

Children can wear their hats on election day.

My Letter to the President!

_____
Date

Dear Mr. President,

_____

_____

_____

_____

_____

_____

_____

_____

_____

_____

_____

_____

Sincerely,

_____

Mail your letter to:
The President of the United States
White House Office
1600 Pennsylvania Ave. N.W.
Washington, D.C. 20500

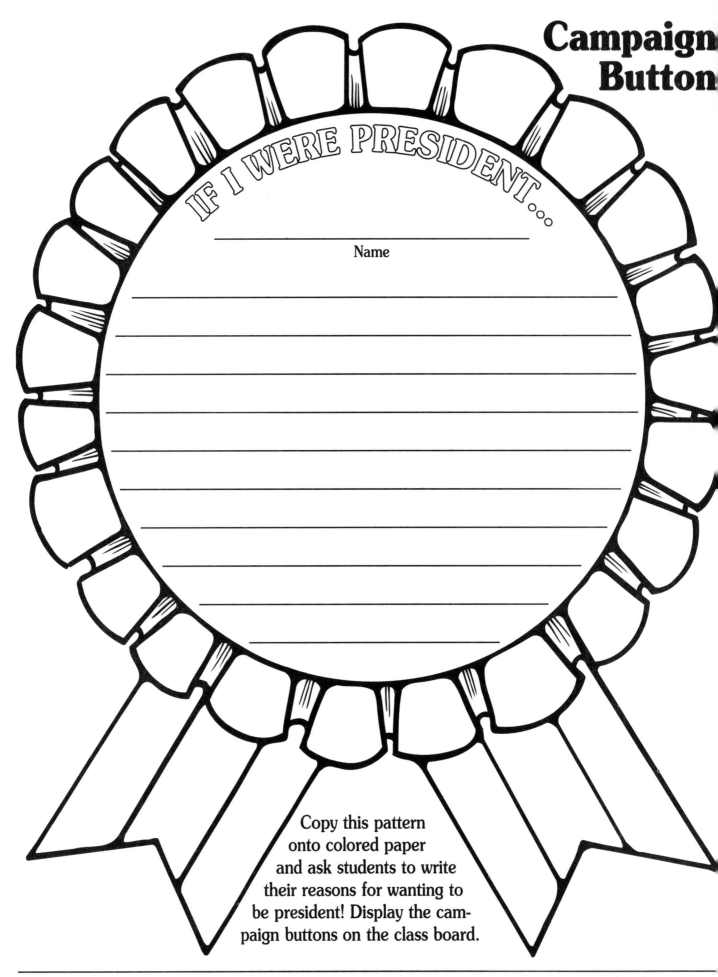

Campaign Button

IF I WERE PRESIDENT...

_____
Name

_____

_____

_____

_____

_____

_____

_____

Copy this pattern onto colored paper and ask students to write their reasons for wanting to be president! Display the campaign buttons on the class board.

President Cards!

These President Cards can be used in a variety of ways in the classroom. Here are a few suggestions:

RESEARCH CARDS

Make a copy of each card, cut them apart and place the cards in a large bowl. Each student draws a card and researches his or her president. Display the research papers next to the picture cards. Here are some questions students can answer about their president:

ORDINAL NUMBERS ACTIVITY

Cover the ordinal number on each President Card. Have students arrange the cards in the order that each president served office.

PRESIDENT CONCENTRATION

Make two copies of each President Card. Have students lay all of the cards face down. Players take turns turning over two cards at a time, matching the presidents. The player with the most pairs wins the game.

BULLETIN BOARD DISPLAY

Display a map of the United States in the center of the class bulletin board. Arrange copies of the President Cards around the map. Use colored yarn to match each President to his home state.

1. Where was your president born and what is his birthdate?
2. How old was your president when he was elected to office?
3. How many years did he serve in office? How many terms?
4. Was your president a Democrat or a Republican? Or neither?
5. Did your president have a nickname? What was it?
6. What was his major contribution while in office?
7. Was he married? Did he have children? How many?
8. Name one major national event that happened during your president's term .

1st

**George Washington
1789-1797**

2nd

John Adams
1797-1801

3rd

Thomas Jefferson
1801-1809

4th

James Madison
1809-1817

5th

James Monroe
1817-1825

6th

John Quincy Adams
1825-1829

7th

Andrew Jackson
1829-1837

8th

Martin Van Buren
1837-1841

9th

William H. Harrison
1841

10th

John Tyler
1841-1845

11th

James K. Polk
1845-1849

12th

Zachary Taylor
1849-1850

13th

Millard Fillmore
1850-1853

14th

Franklin Pierce
1853-1857

15th

James Buchanan
1857-1861

16th

Abraham Lincoln
1861-1865

17th

Andrew Johnson
1865-1869

18th

Ulysses S. Grant
1869-1877

19th

Rutherford B. Hayes
1877-1881

20th

James A. Garfield
1881

21st

Chester A. Arthur
1881-1885

22nd

Grover Cleveland
1885-1889

23rd

Benjamin Harrison
1889-1893

24th

Grover Cleveland
1893-1897

25th

William McKinley
1897-1901

26th
Theodore Roosevelt
1901-1909

27th
William H. Taft
1909-1913

28th
Woodrow Wilson
1913-1921

29th
Warren G. Harding
1921-1923

30th
Calvin Coolidge
1923-1929

31st
Herbert Hoover
1929-1933

32nd

Franklin D. Roosevelt
1933-1945

33rd

Harry S. Truman
1945-1953

34th

Dwight D. Eisenhower
1953-1961

35th

John F. Kennedy
1961-1963

36th

Lyndon B. Johnson
1963-1969

37th

Richard M. Nixon
1969-1974

38th

Gerald R. Ford
1974-1977

39th

Jimmy Carter
1977-1981

40th

Ronald Reagan
1981-1989

41st

George Bush
1989-1993

42nd

William Clinton
1993-2001

43rd

George W. Bush
2001-

My Presidential Report _____

Name

President's Name First Middle Last

Years Served as President [____] to [____] **Republican** [ ]

Democrat [ ]

_____ [ ]

Birthdate _____

Birthplace _____

Home State _____

Nickname _____

Married yes [ ] no [ ] **Spouse's Name** _____

Pets _____ **Children's Names** _____

Vice President _____

Major Contributions: _____

_____

_____

_____

_____

Other Interesting Facts: _____

_____

_____

_____

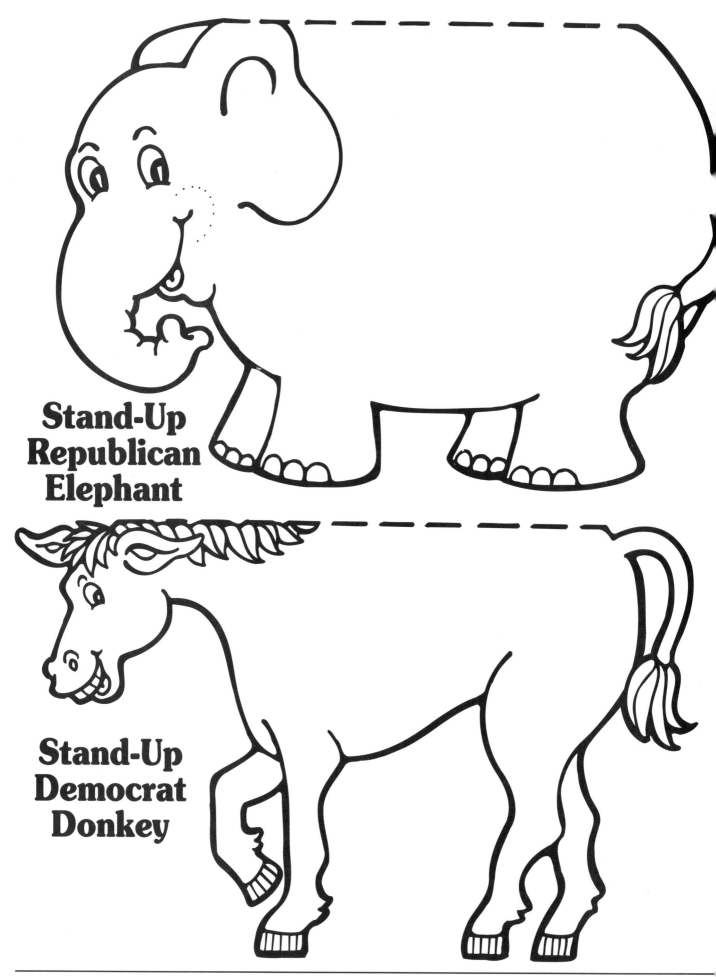

Stand-Up Republican Elephant

Stand-Up Democrat Donkey

Thanksgiving!

The Pilgrim Story!

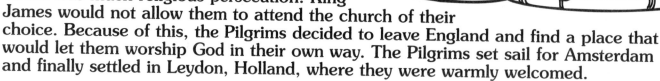

The group of people now known as "Pilgrims" were unhappy about events taking place in their home country of England. There was much religious persecution. King James would not allow them to attend the church of their choice. Because of this, the Pilgrims decided to leave England and find a place that would let them worship God in their own way. The Pilgrims set sail for Amsterdam and finally settled in Leydon, Holland, where they were warmly welcomed.

They soon realized, however, that they could not stay in Holland unless they were willing to give up their English customs and language. The decision was made to set sail for North America where they could establish their own community and preserve the English language.

After much difficulty, they were able to finance and supply two small ships, the "Speedwell" and the "Mayflower." They then began their journey across the Atlantic Ocean. Unfortunately, the "Speedwell" soon began developing a leak and both ships had to return to port. On September 6, 1620, the "Mayflower" set sail alone with 102 people aboard.

This was a difficult time for the Pilgrims. Food was scarce and consisted mostly of salted meat and dry biscuits. They were unable to build fires for either cooking or warmth for fear of burning the ship. Many became ill due to these poor conditions. One happy event did take place during the voyage. A baby was born to the Hopkins family and suitably named "Oceanus."

Land was first sighted on November 11, but it was not until November 21, 1620, that they dropped anchor and began to build a settlement near the present day area of Provincetown, Massachusetts. Before leaving the ship, all of the men signed the "Mayflower Compact," an agreement stating that they were still loyal to the king of England but would set their own laws to provide for their general good and welfare.

Their first winter was extremely difficult. There was little food, and their simple shelters provided little relief from the cold. The Pilgrims quickly made friends with the Indians, who taught them to build stronger houses and hunt for food. When spring finally arrived, the Pilgrims went straight to work plowing the land and planting seeds that they had carried from England. An Indian named Squanto became a very good friend and helped with the planting.

When harvest time came, there were more than enough fruits and vegetables to store for the next winter. The Pilgrims were so thankful that they decided to invite their Indian friends for a feast of thanksgiving.

On the day of the feast, the Pilgrims covered the tables with good things to eat from their gardens. The Indians brought wild turkeys, game and shellfish. Before the feast began, everyone bowed their heads and said a prayer of thanksgiving to God. This first Thanksgiving was a joyous occasion which lasted three days.

Today, Thanksgiving is a legal holiday celebrated on the fourth Thursday of November. In millions of homes across America, families reunite and remember to thank God for all the good that has been given them.

Pilgrim and Indian Activities!

Divide the class into two groups, Pilgrims and Indians. Instruct each student to choose one of these appropriate activities to do. Display the results on the class board during the Thanksgiving season.

PILGRIM ACTIVITIES

1. Make a booklet about the first Thanksgiving and in which you compare it to our own Thanksgiving today.

2. Write a menu for the first Thanksgiving dinner. List the foods in alphabetical order.

3. Research the Mayflower. What was the length of the ship? How many people made the journey? How many days did the trip take?

4. Pretend you are one of the pilgrims. Describe how you are feeling about your new country and write about your experiences during that first year.

5. In your own words, retell the Pilgrim's Thanksgiving story.

(NOTE: Please remember that when teaching about American Indians, it should be done with great respect for their rich culture and heritage.)

INDIAN ACTIVITIES

1. Explain what role the Indians played in helping the pilgrims that first year.

2. Pretend you are an American Indian in the year 1620. You have just seen some strange people coming to shore from a small boat. How do you feel? What do you do?

3. Research the Indians that helped the pilgrims. Describe their community and families. Also explain what clothing they wore and what foods they ate.

4. Draw a picture of an Indian village from the information you have learned.

5. Make a booklet about the Indians at the first Thanksgiving. Compare them to American Indians today.

THANKSGIVING IN THE CLASSROOM
Arrange to have a Thanksgiving feast with several other classrooms. Sharing the contributions will help develop an understanding of the true meaning of Thanksgiving.

Ask each classroom to select a food to prepare and share with the other classrooms. Here are some suggestions:

Popcorn   Pumpkin Pudding   Corn on the Cob
Cranberry Sauce   Corn Bread   Homemade Bread

Pilgrim Girl

Pilgrim Boy

(American Indian boy and girl can be found in the September Idea Book.)

Pilgrim Bonnet and Collar

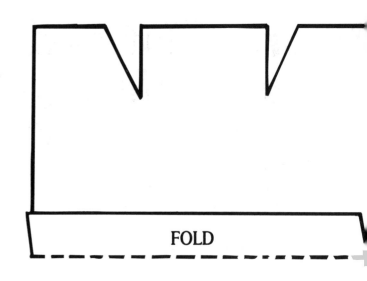

Copy this Pilgrim bonnet onto 12" x 18" white construction paper. Fold over one side, as shown. Bring the back together and staple in place.

Use hair pins to attach to the child's head. Black yarn can also be added to the bonnet and tied under the chin.

FOLD

Staple back ends together.

The collar is also cut from 12" X 18" white construction paper. Fold the paper in half and cut a large circle in the center. Join the front of the collar together with a yarn bow.

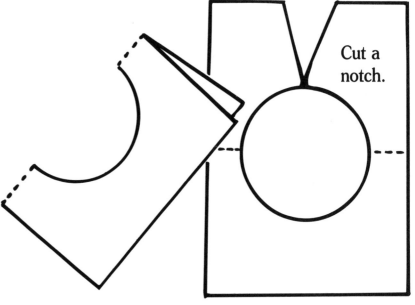

Cut a notch.

Pilgrim Hat and Indian Vest

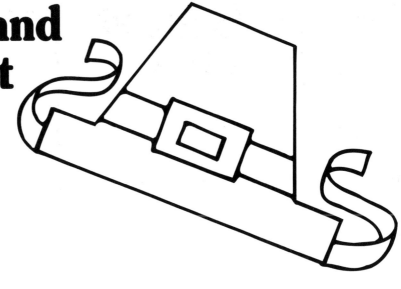

This Pilgrim hat is easily made from 9" x 12" black construction paper. Staple the hat to a paper strip cut to fit a child's head. Add a hat band and a buckle cut from metallic gold adhesive paper.

This simple Indian vest is made from an ordinary grocery bag. Cut a hole for each arm, one for the head and an opening down the front. Children can add their own Indian designs using crayons or paint.

Bags displaying store advertisements can be used by carefully turning them inside-out after you have cut the openings.

Make Indian headbands and feathers from colored construction paper.

Thanksgiving Finger Puppets

Encourage students to act out the first Thanksgiving with these finger puppets.

Cut out

Cut out

Cut out

Cut out

Cut out

Cut out

Cut out

Cut out

Place Cards

Happy Thanksgiving!

_____

- - - - - - - - - - - -

_____

- - - - - - - - - - - -

_____

Copy these place cards onto a folded sheet of heavy paper.
Color, cut out and stand on the Thanksgiving table.

Happy Thanksgiving!

_____

_____

- - - - - - - - - - - -

_____

85

Name

I am most thankful for...

Thanksgiving Characters

Enlarged, these darling characters can be used in bulletin board displays. You might like to make one of them poster board size and attach it to your classroom door. A word of "Welcome" would be all you would need to greet parents during parent-teacher conferences.

These characters can also be used in a flannel board story about Thanksgiving. Cut out and color each illustration. Glue a square of flannel to the back of the picture and apply to the board as you tell the story of the pilgrims.

The pilgrims gave thanks to God for their many blessings.

With the help of the Indians, the pilgrims built strong houses.

During the long voyage on the Mayflower, a baby was born to the Hopkins family and appropriately named "Oceanus."

Squanto helped the pilgrims with the planting, fishing and hunting. He became a very good friend.

At harvest time, there were more than enough fruits and vegetables to store for the winter.

The Mayflower

On September 6, 162 the "Mayflower" set sa alone with 102 people aboard.

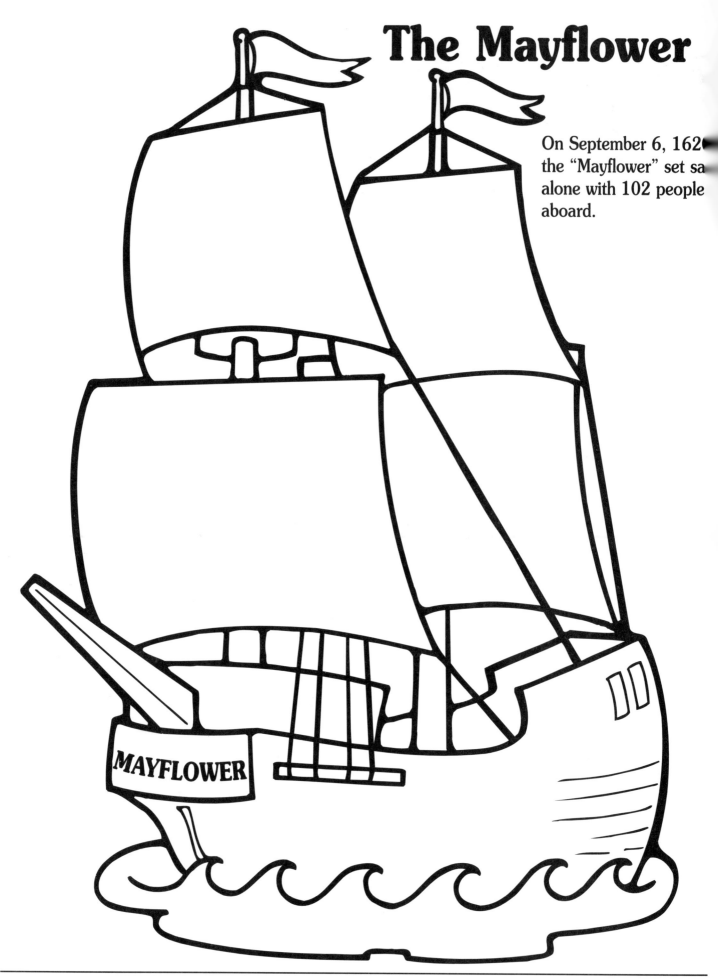

MAYFLOWER

Turkey Time!

Turkey Time Activities!

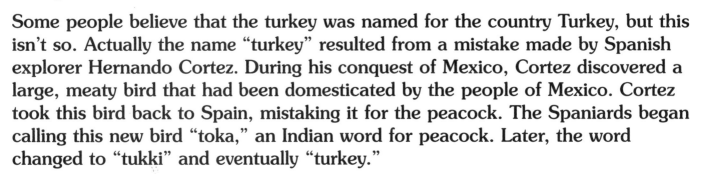

The North American wild turkey was native to our land long before the arrival of the Pilgrims. These wild turkeys were a vital source of food and clothing for many of the East Coast Indians. Turkey feathers were also used to make arrows.

These early American turkeys were much different than the domesticated turkeys of today. These wild turkeys were tough, sinewy birds that had to fly to survive. It took many careful hours of cooking to make the meat tender enough to eat.

Some people believe that the turkey was named for the country Turkey, but this isn't so. Actually the name "turkey" resulted from a mistake made by Spanish explorer Hernando Cortez. During his conquest of Mexico, Cortez discovered a large, meaty bird that had been domesticated by the people of Mexico. Cortez took this bird back to Spain, mistaking it for the peacock. The Spaniards began calling this new bird "toka," an Indian word for peacock. Later, the word changed to "tukki" and eventually "turkey."

The Spaniards gradually bred the birds to be more meaty and tender. It is said that the turkey was "one of the most beautiful presents which the New World has given to the Old." Today, more than 500 million turkeys a year find their way to our Thanksgiving tables.

TURKEY TASKS
1. Write the directions for cooking a Thanksgiving turkey. List specific ingredients as well as cooking times and temperature.
2. Describe what Thanksgiving dinner will be like in the year 2050.
3. Write a thank you note to the member of your family that hosted your Thanksgiving feast.
4. Imagine that you can ask anyone in the world to your Thanksgiving dinner. Who would you invite and why?
5. Write a paragraph on today's turkeys and how they are different from the ones eaten at the first Thanksgiving.
6. To "talk turkey" means to speak bluntly. Write three "talk turkey" sentences about turkeys.
7. Using ads from the newspaper, plan a Thanksgiving feast for your family. Find the price of each item you would need to buy. Add up your total to find the cost of your Thanksgiving meal.

Turkey Booklet

Turkey Centerpiece

Cut out the turkey patterns and color with crayons. Fold the turkey head at the dotted line.

Use a potato for the turkey's body. Cut a small flat spot on the bottom of a potato to keep it from rolling. Attach the head, wings and tail with toothpicks.

Set several turkeys on the Thanksgiving table as creative centerpieces.

You can also enlarge these patterns and use a pumpkin as the turkey's body!

Turkey Feathers

I'm thankful for...

isplay the turkeys
n the class bulletin
oard. Students can
dd the "I'm thankful
or..." feathers to
heir own turkey!

Name

Mr. Turkey

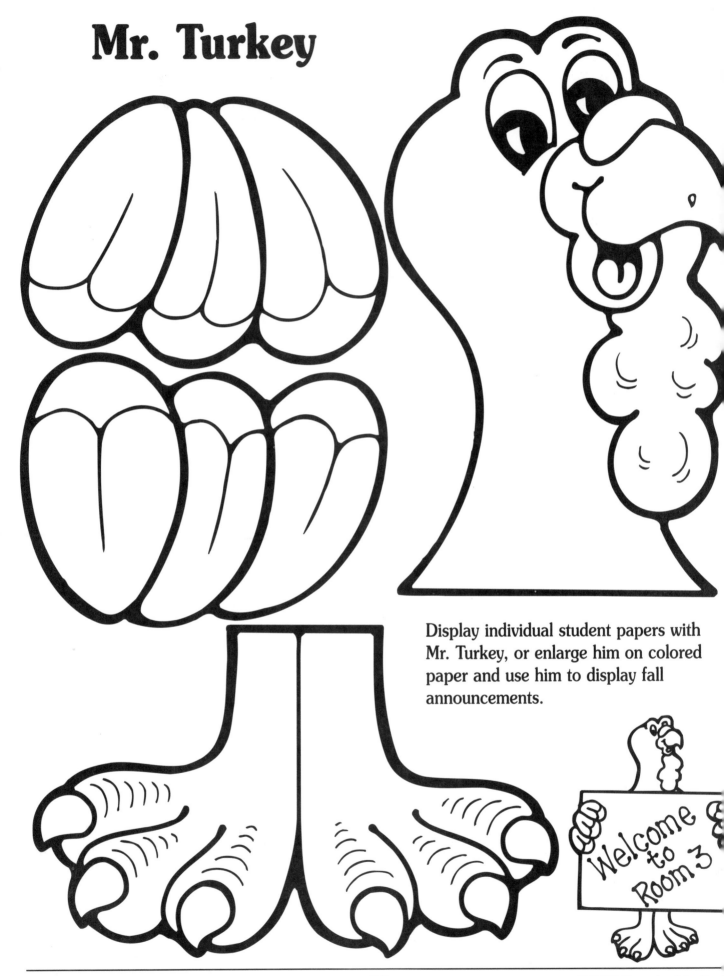

Display individual student papers with Mr. Turkey, or enlarge him on colored paper and use him to display fall announcements.

Welcome to Room 3

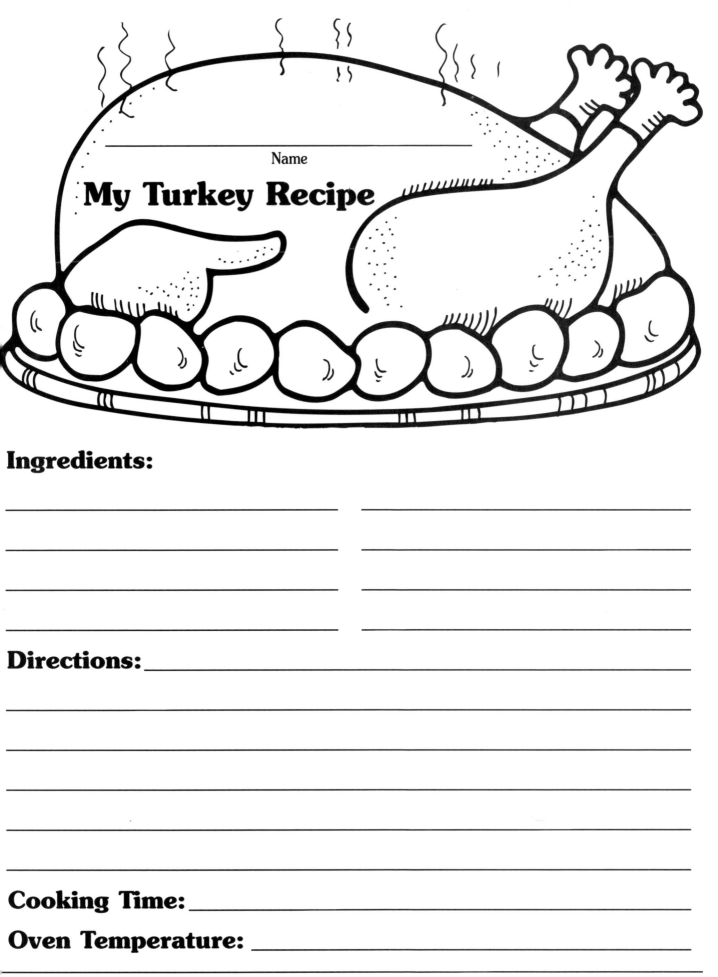

Name

My Turkey Recipe

Ingredients:

_____   _____

_____   _____

_____   _____

_____   _____

Directions: _____

_____

_____

_____

_____

_____

Cooking Time: _____

Oven Temperature: _____

Turkey Wheel

Cut out

Cut out

Cut out
these pat-
terns and
assemble this
"Turkey Wheel" with
a brass fastener. Cut out
the two rectangles, as shown.

Add your own math problems and answers to the wheel. Move the turkey wing to reveal the answer.

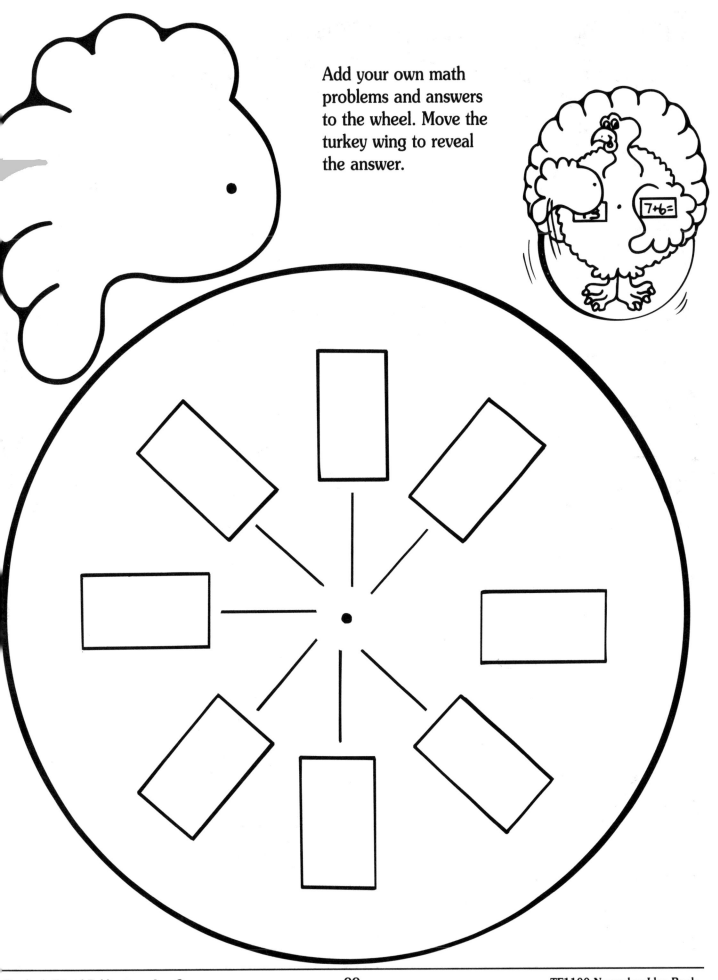

7+6=

Moveable Turkey

Cut these turkey patterns from colored construction paper and color with crayons. Assemble with brass fasteners.

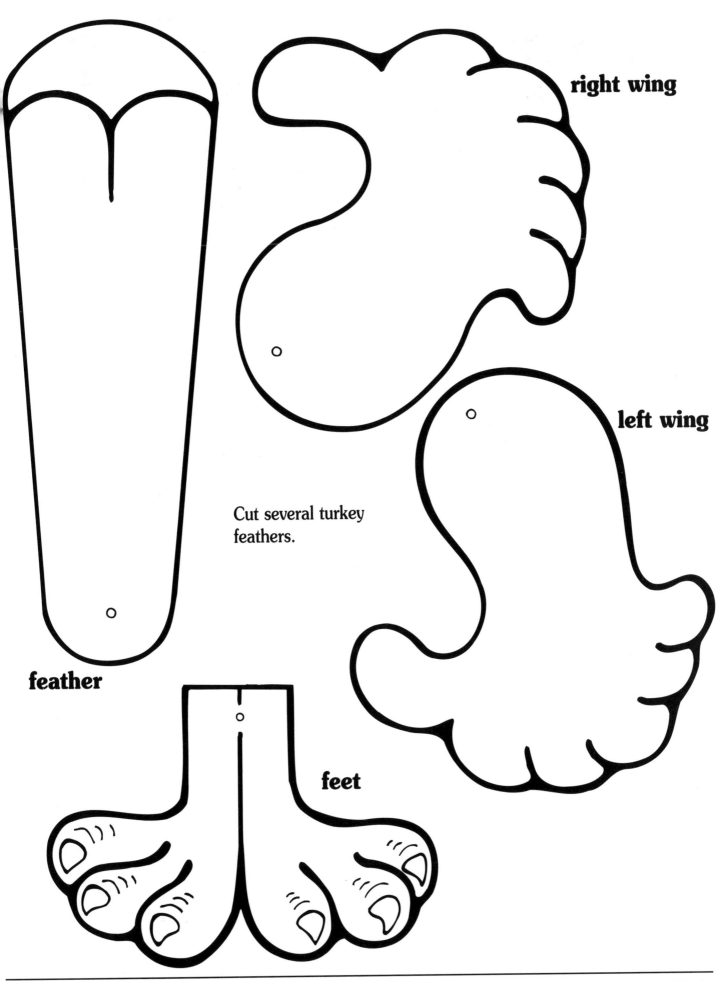

right wing

left wing

Cut several turkey feathers.

feather

feet

Turkey Paper Bag Puppet

Cut these pattern pieces to a small lunch bag to make a cute turkey puppet.

Children may want to cut feathers from colored paper and glue them to the back of the bag.

States and Capitals!

States and Capitals Activities!

Fifty individual states make up the United States of America. Each state is unique in its own way. Help your students to learn the geographical location of the states and capitals and appreciate their many differences. Try some of these activities with your students.

STATE NAMES - Have students research the origin of each state name. Some state names can be traced to Indian cultures, such as North and South Dakota. Other states were named for people, such as Pennsylvania for William Penn, the area's first leader. Ask children to write brief paragraphs that can be posted by the state's name on the class bulletin board.

STATE NICKNAMES - Each state has an official or unofficial nickname. Florida is "The Sunshine State" and California is "The Golden State." Assign a state to each student and have them find out their state's nickname. Ask them to find out why this name was chosen and whether or not it seems appropriate. Have them to come up with some other nicknames that might be more suitable.

COLOR THE U.S. - Give each child a blank map of the United States. Direct them to find various states by listening to your clues, such as "Alabama touches the Gulf of Mexico. Color it green." Or, "The State of Oregon is on the Pacific Coast. Color it blue." This is a fun way to learn the location and names of all fifty states.

STATE CAPITAL BEE - Using the same rules as a Spelling Bee, divide your class into teams. Verbally give each participant the name of a state. They must correctly identify the capital or leave the game and be seated. Proceed until one team is the winner. Change the game by giving the capitals and having the students answer with the names of the states. This is a fun way to motivate students to learn their states and capitals.

STATES AND CAPITALS BINGO - This is an exciting way to practice memorizing the states and their capitals. Give each child a copy of the states or capitals or write their names on the chalkboard. Ask students to write any 24 names on his or her bingo card. Use the same directions you might use for regular bingo. (List of states and capitals can be found on page 144.)

STATE FOLDERS - As a cover for state reports, have students fold a large sheet of construction paper in half and draw an outline of their state on one side. Insert lined paper inside and staple along the folded edge. Cut the booklets along the remaining three sides. Children can then write their state reports inside the folder.

My State Report On:

Student's Name

My state is:

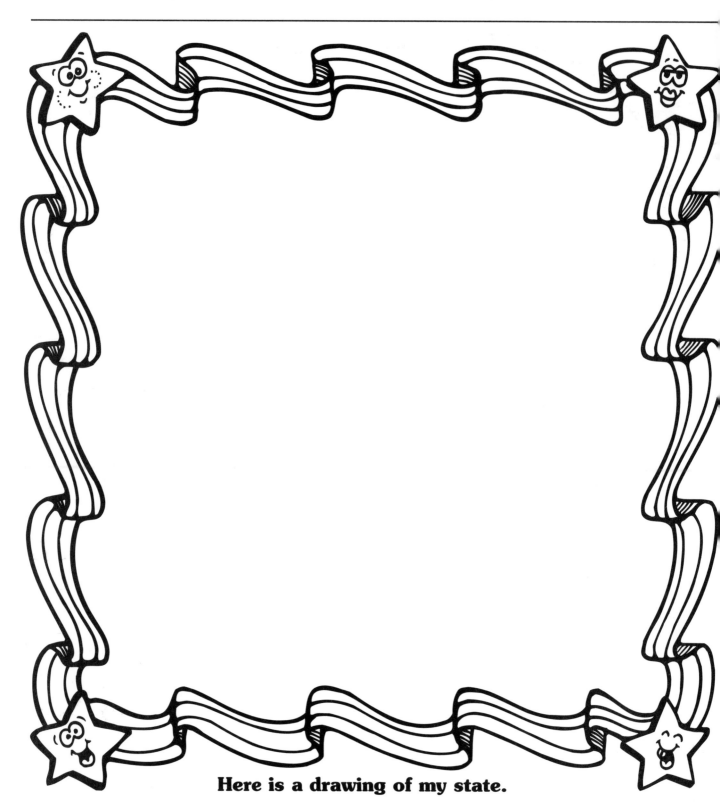

Here is a drawing of my state.

My state's capital is:

State Flag

Three of my state's resources:

1. _____

2. _____

3. _____

My state is located:

☐ **In the West**   ☐ **In the Northeast**

☐ **In the Midwest**   ☐ **In the Southwest**

☐ **In the South**   ☐ **Somewhere else**

(Color your state.)

Here is my state!

My state is bordered by: _____

_____

_____

_____

_____

My state's nickname is:

_____

_____

My state was admitted to the Union in:_____

There are about _____ people that live in my state.

My state flower is:

_____

My state bird is:

_____

My state's motto is: _____

_____

_____

_____

My state is famous for many things.
Here are a few:

1. _____

2. _____

3. _____

4. _____

5. _____

A famous person from my state is:

_____

_____

He or she is famous for:

_____

_____

_____

_____

_____

_____

_____

(His or Her picture.)

Year born [   ]   **Year died** [   ]

My state's main rivers, lakes and mountains are:

_____

_____

_____

_____

Historically, my state is famous for:

_____

_____

_____

_____

_____

The reasons to visit my state are:

_____

_____

_____

_____

_____

_____

Identify each state by listing them 1 through 50.

United States of America Map

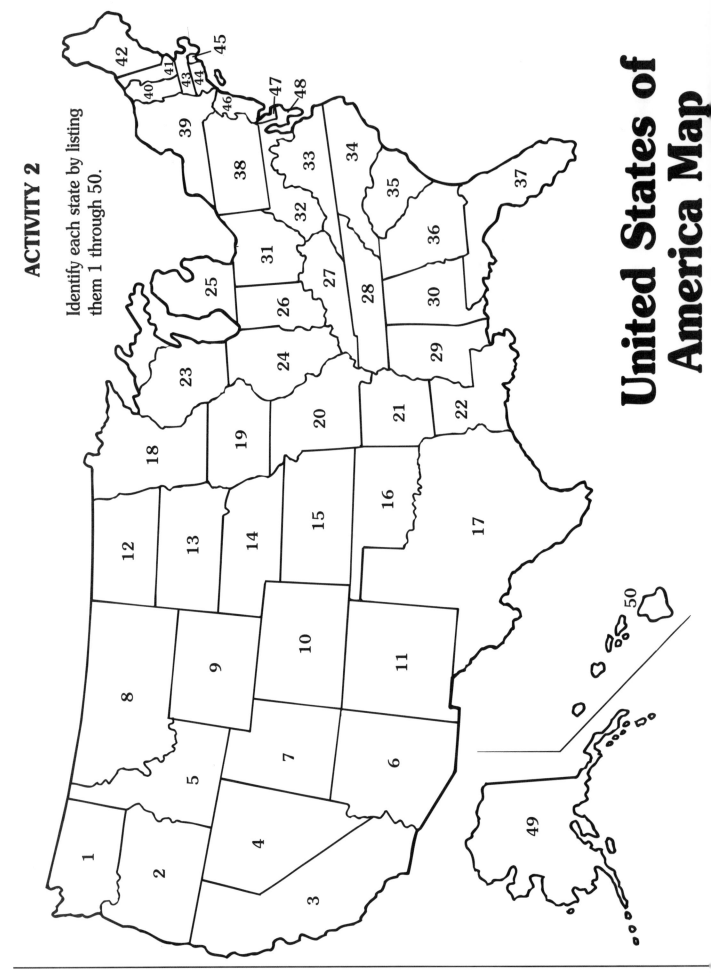

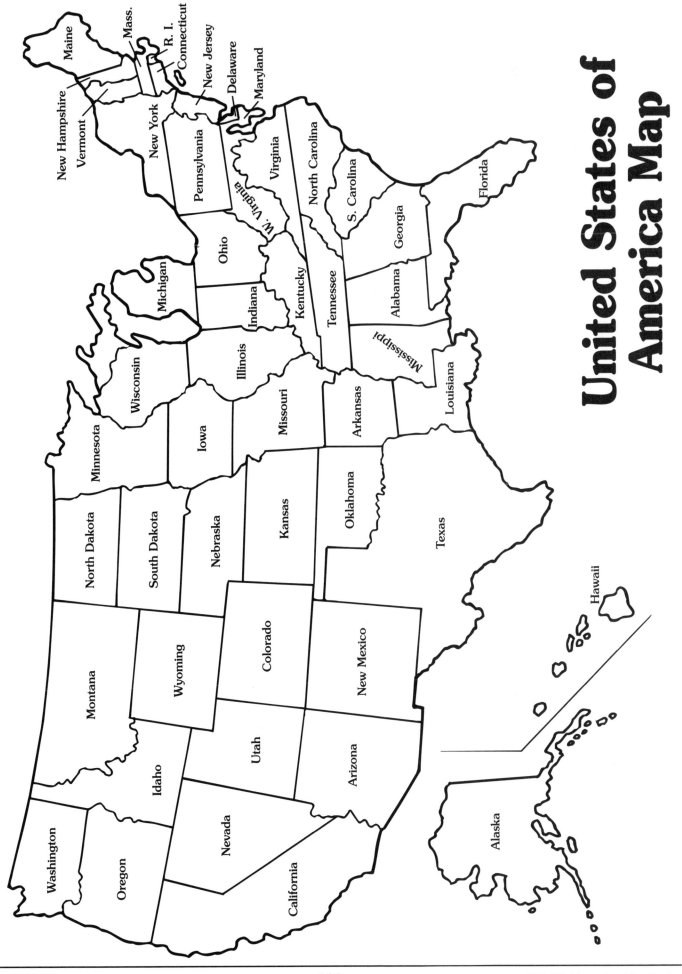

United States of America Map

Maine
New Hampshire
Vermont
Mass.
R. I.
Connecticut
New Jersey
Delaware
Maryland
New York
Pennsylvania
W. Virginia
Virginia
North Carolina
S. Carolina
Florida
Ohio
Kentucky
Tennessee
Alabama
Georgia
Michigan
Indiana
Mississippi
Wisconsin
Illinois
Missouri
Arkansas
Louisiana
Minnesota
Iowa
North Dakota
South Dakota
Nebraska
Kansas
Oklahoma
Texas
Montana
Wyoming
Colorado
New Mexico
Idaho
Utah
Arizona
Washington
Oregon
Nevada
California
Alaska
Hawaii

STATES AND CAPITALS
BINGO

FREE

Working With Parents!

Note: Check out Teacher's Friend Parent-Teacher Conference Essential Folder for more resources contained in a fun organizational folder.

- Conferences!
- Open House!
- Communications!

Ideas for Parent-Teacher Conferences, Open House and Parent Communications!

PARENT-PUPIL POTLUCK!

Get parents involved with school with this yummy idea!

With your students' input, select a date and potluck theme. Have the children design an invitation and ask them to take it home to their parents. Students with last names beginning A-J bring a salad, K-R bring a main dish and S-Z brings a dessert. Ask each family to provide their own paper products and cutlery. You can provide paper cups and punch. By getting to know you and other parents better, your students' parents will be eager to help out at school and get more involved in their child's school experience.

OPEN HOUSE GOODIE BAGS!

Give each student a brightly-colored lunch bag. Ask them to decorate the bags for their parents to take during Open House. Fill the bags with good work papers, a special note students write to their parents and any small art projects. At the close of the day, after the classroom is spruced-up and desks straightened, have students set the bags on their desk tops. Parents will be proud to take the bags home to share with other family members.

PARENT SIGN-UP SHEETS!

Encourage students to help in the classroom, especially during holidays and field trips by sending home a parent sign-up sheet. (A sample form is contained in this unit.) Add known dates or any other specific information before duplicating the form for your students.

UP-LIFTING OPEN HOUSE

At your local gift store, have a large balloon filled with helium and tied with a ribbon to give to each child in class. (You may wish to have several extra balloons filled, just in case some break unexpectedly.) Give each student a balloon and ask them to write their names on the balloons using a permanent marker. Tie the appropriate balloon to each student's desk. What an "uplifting" and colorful way to welcome parents to class! (Parents can then take the balloon home to their child after the conferences.)

MYSTERY STUDENT!

Break the ice during Open House or Parent-Teacher Conferences with a "Mystery Student" bulletin board. Give each student the "Mystery Student" questionnaire to fill out. Frame the papers with colorful paper and display them on the class board. As parents visit the classroom, ask them to guess which questionnaire was filled out by their child. Parents can then write the student's name at the bottom of the page.

CLASSROOM UPDATE!

Send weekly or bi-weekly update notices home to parents using the form in this unit. Fill in the important information you wish to send to parents, duplicate on colored paper and send a copy home with each student on a regular basis.

This quick wayof notifying parents of classroom achievements and upcoming events will go a long way in your efforts to communicate with your students' parents.

Classroom Update!

Teacher _____ Room # _____

School _____ Date _____

Look What's Happening!

_____
_____
_____
_____
_____
_____
_____
_____
_____
_____
_____

Special Students!

_____
_____
_____
_____
_____
_____
_____
_____
_____
_____
_____

Upcoming Events! _____
_____
_____

How Parents Can Help! _____
_____
_____

Here's How to Contact the Teacher! _____
_____
_____

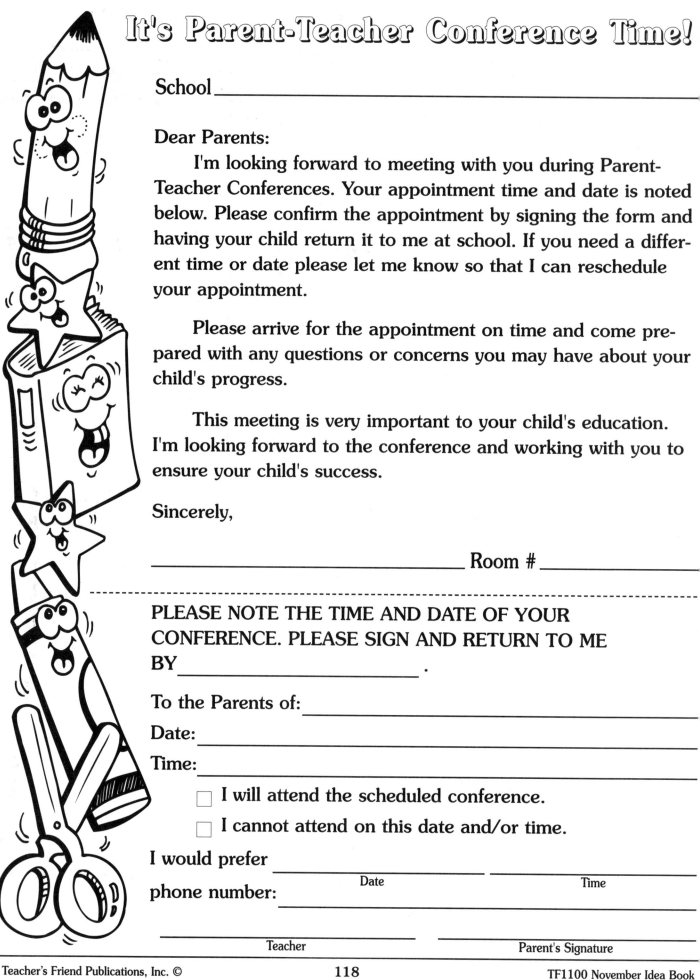

It's Parent-Teacher Conference Time!

School _____

Dear Parents:

   I'm looking forward to meeting with you during Parent-Teacher Conferences. Your appointment time and date is noted below. Please confirm the appointment by signing the form and having your child return it to me at school. If you need a different time or date please let me know so that I can reschedule your appointment.

   Please arrive for the appointment on time and come prepared with any questions or concerns you may have about your child's progress.

   This meeting is very important to your child's education. I'm looking forward to the conference and working with you to ensure your child's success.

Sincerely,

_____ Room # _____

- -

PLEASE NOTE THE TIME AND DATE OF YOUR CONFERENCE. PLEASE SIGN AND RETURN TO ME BY_____ .

To the Parents of: _____

Date: _____

Time: _____

☐ I will attend the scheduled conference.

☐ I cannot attend on this date and/or time.

I would prefer _____ _____
                        Date   Time

phone number: _____

_____   _____
      Teacher   Parent's Signature

Parents!
You're Invited
to our
OPEN HOUSE!

Date: _____

Time: _____

Teacher: _____

Room #: _____

Parent-Teacher Conference Individual Student Check List

(Here are a few suggestions for discussing individual students' achievements, abilities and concerns.)

- Greet the parent(s) and express your pleasure in their attendance at the conference.

- Tell the parent(s) how much you enjoy having their child in class and give an example.

- Show several samples of the student's work covering various areas of the curriculum.

- Thoroughly discuss the student's report card, ask for questions and comments and give the parent(s) a copy to take home.

- Supply the parents with a copy of your school's manuscript or cursive alphabet.

- Give parent(s) a list of suggestions outlining how they can help the child at home.

- Explain your discipline policy and homework procedures.

- Provide documentation of the student's absences.

- Have handy a copy of each text or reading book you may wish to discuss.

- Discuss any problems concerning the student's relationship with others, work habits, motivation and attitude.

- Discuss any health concerns such as sight problems, nutrition, need for adequate sleep, etc.

- Ask parents to write a brief, positive note to their child that can be left in his or her desk and found the next day.

- End the conference on a positive note by summarizing the highlights of the meeting and thanking the parents for coming and being involved in their child's school experience.

Parent Reminder!

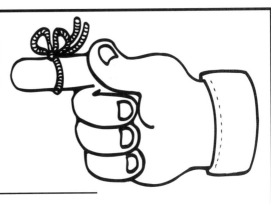

Just a reminder that you have volunteered to _____

_____

on _____

Thank you so much for your help!

_____   _____
            Teacher   Room #

I'm the proud parent of:

_____

My name is:

_____

_____

Dear Parent:
Your child is the greatest!
I especially enjoy.....

_____

_____

_____

_____

Signed,

_____
Your child's teacher

Parent-Teacher Communications

Student: _____

READING

MATH

LANGUAGE ARTS

SCIENCE

SOCIAL SCIENCE

WORK HABITS

HOMEWORK

(Teachers or Parents can use this sheet to record comments or concerns about a student's abilities and participation in various school subjects.)

PARENT SIGN-UP SHEET

Teacher_____ Room #_____

Please sign up for ways you can help during the school year, such as bake cookies, providing paper products, helping in the classroom, supervising field trips, etc. Please send this form back to school with your child.

Halloween Party! Student's Name:_____
Parent's Name:_____ Phone:_____
Ways I can help!_____
_____

Christmas Party! Student's Name:_____
Parent's Name:_____ Phone:_____
Ways I can help!_____
_____

Valentine's Party! Student's Name:_____
Parent's Name:_____ Phone:_____
Ways I can help!_____
_____

Easter Party! Student's Name:_____
Parent's Name:_____ Phone:_____
Ways I can help!_____
_____

Year-End Party! Student's Name:_____
Parent's Name:_____ Phone:_____
Ways I can help!_____
_____

Field Trips! Approximate Dates:_____
Student's Name:_____
Parent's Name:_____ Phone:_____
Ways I can help!_____

Mystery Student!

I am a ☐ **Boy** ☐ **Girl**

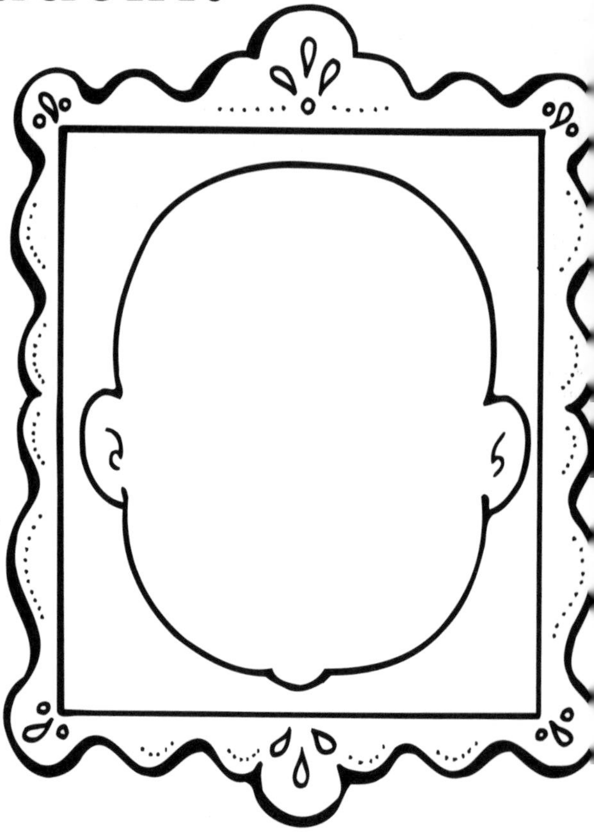

I have _____ eyes!

I have _____ hair!

My favorite color is _____ .

I have _____ sisters
   and _____ brothers.

My Portrait!

My best friend is:

_____

My favorite school subjects are _____

_____

My favorite thing to do is _____

_____

I also love to _____

_____

But I don't like to _____

_____

Guess Who I Am!

_____
Name

A Note to My Child!

A Note to My Parent!

Signed

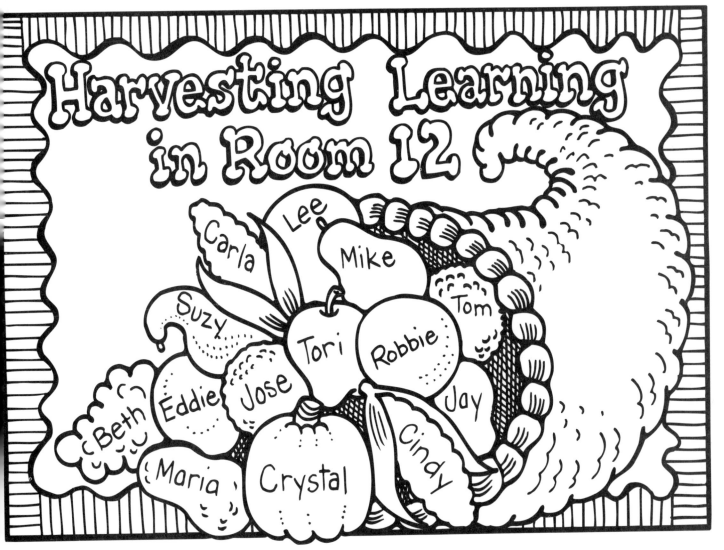

Harvesting Learning in Room 12

Bulletin Boards and More!

THE STUFFIN'S IN THE LIBRARY

Display a large paper turkey on the class bulletin board for a clever library display.

Children can display book reports or student-made book jackets.

HANDS-DOWN TURKEY

This delightful turkey will take center stage in your classroom. Enlarge the turkey's head and feet onto posterboard and cut them out. Ask students to trace both of their hands and feet on red, yellow and orange construction paper. The cut-out prints can be pinned to the board to form the turkey's body and tail, as illustrated.

Depending on the number of prints you wish to make, you can make the turkey as large or small as you want.

FEAST OF WORDS

What a great way to introduce November vocabulary words!

Students will love finding "tasty" words to display on this "delicious" bulletin board.

A long scroll of white butcher paper can be used to title the "Feast of Words."

Bulletin Boards and More!

ELECTION TIME

Use red, white and blue striped gift-wrapping paper for this patriotic bulletin board. Students can display presidential reports or campaign buttons.

(If you already have a board covered with either blue or red butcher paper, simply pin strips of white paper over the existing covering.)

PILGRIM AND INDIAN FACES

Let your students draw self-portraits on the back of white paper plates. Headbands, feathers, pilgrim hats and bonnets can be cut from colored construction paper. Make sure that each child adds his or her own name to the finished product. This is a clever way to involve your students in welcoming the Thanksgiving holiday.

PILGRIM FACTS

Display a large paper-cut "Mayflower" on the class bulletin board.

Ask students to research facts about the Pilgrims. Have them write their findings on strips of paper and display them on the board.

(If you have planned ahead, you can use the same ship for an "Explorers" display. Simply remove the name "Mayflower.")

Bulletin Boards and More!

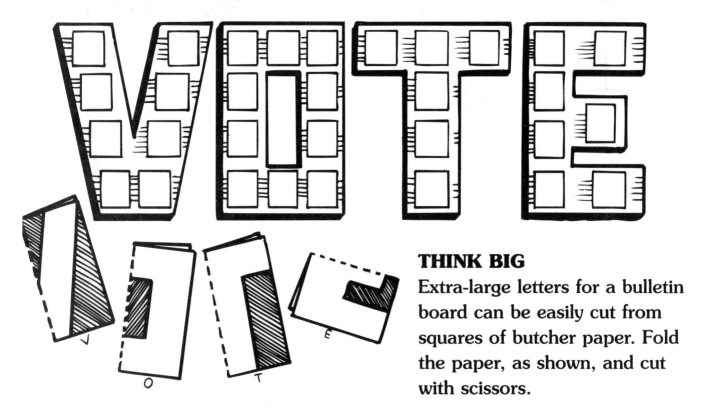

THINK BIG

Extra-large letters for a bulletin board can be easily cut from squares of butcher paper. Fold the paper, as shown, and cut with scissors.

Try the word MAPS for map studies, MATH for excellent work and ZOO for animal reports.

A GREAT NATION

Display a large white scroll cut from butcher paper on the class bulletin board. Children can write papers explaining the need for good citizenship and love for our country.

A GREAT NATION STARTS WITH ONE PERSON... YOU!

Hands-Down
Turkey Pattern

(Add the hands and feet
cut-outs as shown on
page 128.)

Student Helpers

Flag Salute

Mark

Give one boy or girl helper pattern to each child in class. The children can do their own coloring and cutting. Ask them to print their own name on either the bow or the baseball cap.

Label small envelopes with the names of classroom duties. Pin them to the class bulletin board. Slip the cute boy/girl helpers into the appropriate duty envelopes. Switch them weekly so that each child can be included.

Thanksgiving Feast Patterns

(Introduce new vocabulary words with these patterns as shown on page 128.)

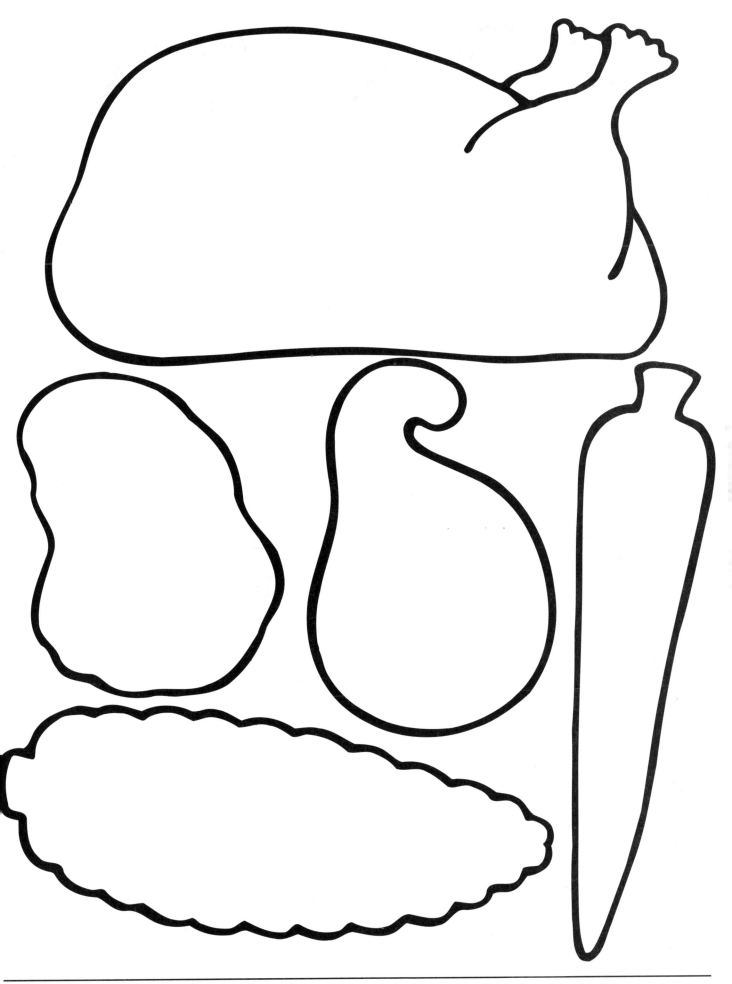

Mayflower Pattern

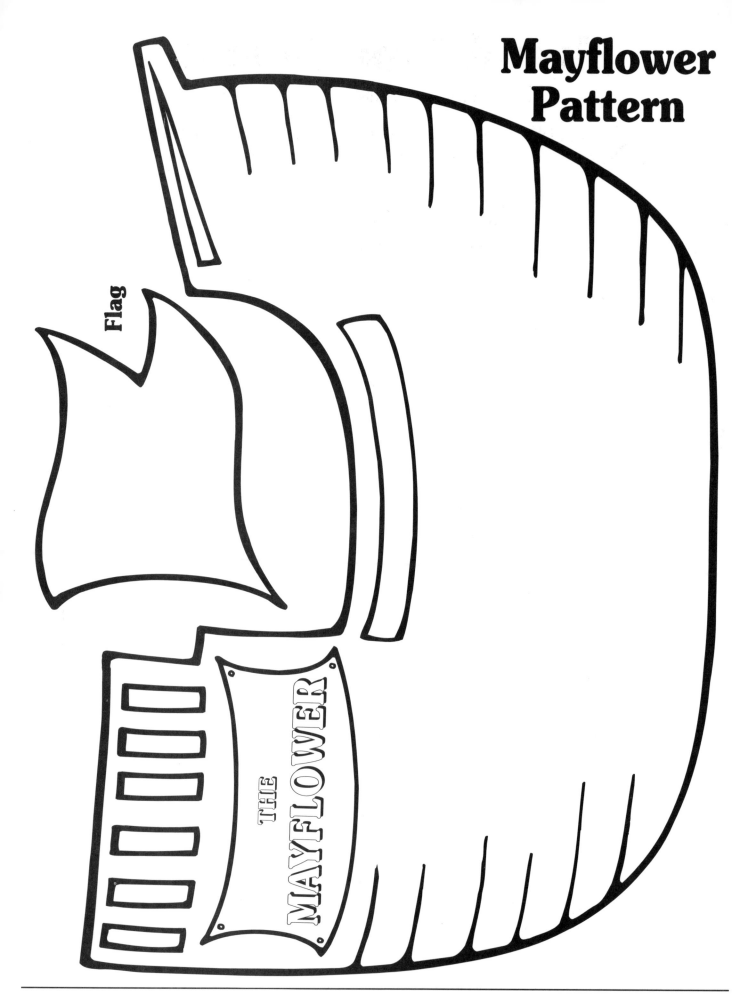

Flag

THE MAYFLOWER

Award Paper Topper

Here's a cute way to display students' work!

Cut these Paper Toppers from colored paper. Or, students can color them with crayons or markers.

Fold along the dotted lines, tape the back together and insert over the corner of a student's good work paper! Display the papers with the toppers on the class board.

WOW!

Apple Paper Topper

Star Paper Topper

You can also reduce the size of these cute paper toppers and use them as unique book marks.

Award them to students when a determined number of pages have been read!

Paper Bag Eagle

This majestic eagle is easily made with a small paper lunch bag. Fill the bag with crumpled paper and close with a rubber band.

Color and cut out the eagle head and two wing patterns and glue to the bag.

Display the eagles on the class bulletin board for a "high flying" display.

Indian Chief

Have students cut out, color and paste this Indian Chief to construction paper. Pupils can fill out a headdress feather, request the teacher's signature and affix it to the chief's headband. Students will love to see how many feathers they can collect.

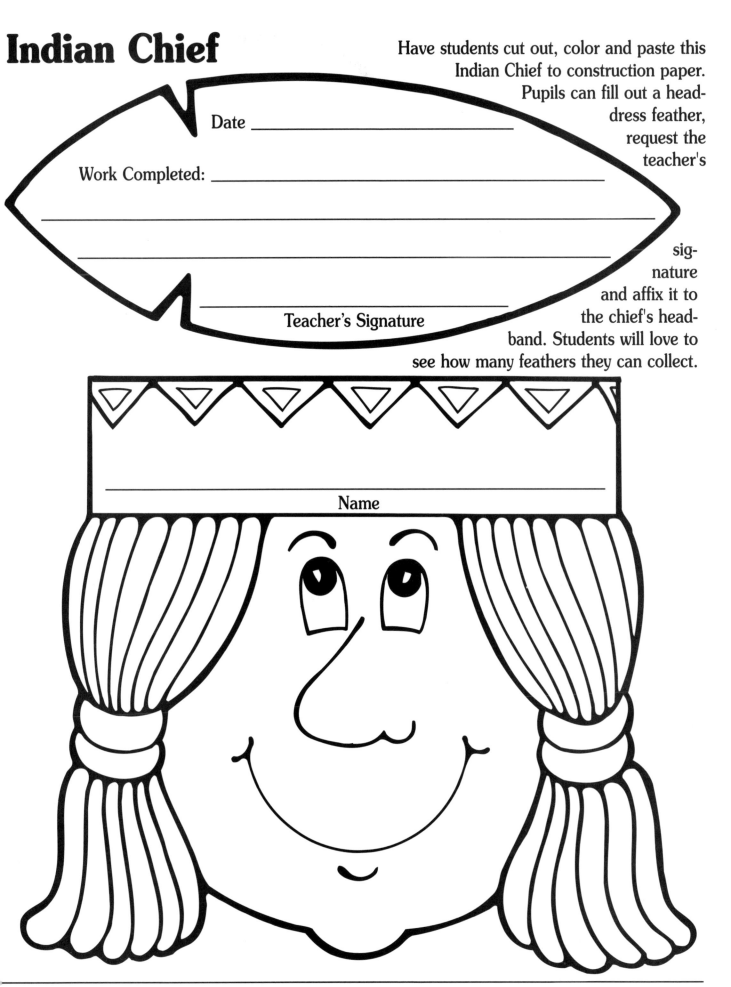

Date _____

Work Completed: _____

_____

_____

_____
Teacher's Signature

Name _____

Gobble, Gobble!

Use this "hungry" turkey to display creative stories or good work papers.

You may wish to enlarge him to bulletin board size and place him over the classroom door. Or, display him on the class board with the title "We're Gobbling Up Subtraction Facts" or "What a Feast of Learning!"

Answer Key!

ACTIVITY 1

FIND THESE ELECTION WORDS: NOVEMBER, PRESIDENT, VICE-PRESIDENT, VOTE, BALLOT, DEMOCRAT, REPUBLICAN, CANDIDATE, SPEECH, CAMPAIGN, CONVENTION, INAUGURATION, ELECTION, TERM, NATION.

```
S V R T G H Y K L H N S P E E C H F B N K L Y
X Z A S W Q R T H Y B H R D C V T Y H U J M H
D C X V C A N D I D A T E F H J I I L K M N G
V F G H O S X V B H L J S F T Y N A T I O N P
W R T Y N C H Y U I L N I B G H A R Y U I O P
C V G Y V H U I K J O R D S W E U C V C W Q E
Q S X D E G B F D R T U E D S W G F R A F V B
M L K O N O V E M B E R N O K J U J K M F G T
E L E C T I O N D R T Y T H N J R H G P C V B
R T Y U I S R T G H U J K I O L A G H A C X Z
L P O I O G F D E M O C R A T F T A W I D R T
S G H U N G H Y U I K M N H U Y I F T G E W Y
V I C E P R E S I D E N T F G T O F N N C E T
O F R H G B N M K I L O H B G Y N R F D E W S
T E R M C D F R E P U B L I C A N F R H Y U K
E S C V T G B N J U I K M K L O P M N J H Y T
X D R T G V B H U J M N H Y T R E W Q A S D E
F R G B N J I U H J K L O P M N B V G F R Q W
```

ACTIVITY 2

1. Washington
2. Oregon
3. California
4. Nevada
5. Idaho
6. Arizona
7. Utah
8. Montana
9. Wyoming
10. Colorado
11. New Mexico
12. North Dakota
13. South Dakota
14. Nebraska
15. Kansas
16. Oklahoma
17. Texas
18. Minnesota
19. Iowa
20. Missouri
21. Arkansas
22. Louisiana
23. Wisconsin
24. Illinois
25. Michigan

26. Indiana
27. Kentucky
28. Tennessee
29. Mississippi
30. Alabama
31. Ohio
32: West Virginia
33. Virginia
34. North Carolina
35. South Carolina
36. Georgia
37. Florida
38. Pennsylvania
39. New York
40. Vermont
41. New Hampshire
42. Maine
43. Massachusetts
44. Connecticut
45. Rhode Island
46. New Jersey
47. Delaware
48. Maryland
49. Alaska
50. Hawaii

Answer Key!

STATES AND CAPITALS

Alabama	Montgomery	New York	Albany
Alaska	Juneau	North Carolina	Raleigh
Arizona	Phoenix	North Dakota	Bismark
Arkansas	Little Rock	Ohio	Columbus
California	Sacramento	Oklahoma	Oklahoma City
Colorado	Denver	Oregon	Salem
Connecticut	Hartford	Pennsylvania	Harrisburg
Delaware	Dover	Rhode Island	Providence
Florida	Tallahassee	South Carolina	Columbia
Georgia	Atlanta	South Dakota	Pierre
Hawaii	Honolulu	Tennessee	Nashville
Idaho	Boise	Texas	Austin
Illinois	Springfield	Utah	Salt Lake City
Indiana	Indianapolis	Vermont	Montpelier
Iowa	Des Moines	Virginia	Richmond
Kansas	Topeka	Washington	Olympia
Kentucky	Frankfort	West Virginia	Charleston
Louisiana	Baton Rouge	Wisconsin	Madison
Maine	Augusta	Wyoming	Cheyenne
Maryland	Annapolis		
Massachusetts	Boston		
Michigan	Lansing		
Minnesota	St. Paul		
Mississippi	Jackson		
Missouri	Jefferson City		
Montana	Helena		
Nebraska	Lincoln		
Nevada	Carson City		
New Hampshire	Concord		
New Jersey	Trenton		
New Mexico	Santa Fe